# HUNTER SUTHERLAND'S
# SLAVE MANUMISSIONS AND SALES
# IN
# HARFORD COUNTY, MARYLAND
# 1775-1865

Carolyn Greenfield Adams

## HERITAGE BOOKS
2007

# HERITAGE BOOKS
## *AN IMPRINT OF HERITAGE BOOKS, INC.*

**Books, CDs, and more—Worldwide**

For our listing of thousands of titles see our website
at
www.HeritageBooks.com

Published 2007 by
HERITAGE BOOKS, INC.
Publishing Division
65 East Main Street
Westminster, Maryland 21157-5026

International Standard Book Number: 978-0-7884-1144-1

## *DEDICATION*

To my mother, Mary Eva Anderson Greenfield, who passed on to me her thirst for learning, love for humanity and appreciation for our Harford County home.

# TABLE OF CONTENTS

# PREFACE

Early workers in the vineyard of African American Genealogy found that they had a *tough row to hoe*. Once one had researched and documented a family to 1865, it was held that to go beyond that point was an impossibility. It was widely held that records did not exist. In many instances persistence, patience and perseverance by researchers has proven to the contrary. Records, supposedly lost or non-existent have been found in the Library of Congress, the National Archives, and in the holdings of local Genealogical and Historical Societies.

Manumission records have proven to be in this category. In many instances manumission records and certificates of freedom have been found to contain invaluable clues to the past of African Americans. They have been found to contain statements of relationship, location of individuals or families, dates of birth, ages and occupations thus leading the researcher a step or two down the trail to ancestors.

These records, when combined with census statistics and other data related to their time period also give further insight into the prevalent social and economic conditions. Such study yields a greater understanding of society in its totality as opposed to its African American segment.

With these points in mind, the reader is encouraged to utilize the abstracts herein contained as a jumping off point and a guide to original documents. Consultation of this work combined with examination of the originals will prove an enriching experience.

Finally, those of us who are laboring in the field welcome this work as part of an ever-growing body of knowledge. We hope that its success will encourage our author to continue her labors.

Jerry M. Hynson
October 1998

# FOREWARD

Hunter C. Sutherland, an historian by interest and education, became involved in what was then called black history during the Civil Rights movement of the 1960s and 70s. Finding little in print of manumission records, he set about to collect what information he could from the extant historical records of Harford County including wills, property inventories and military records.

It is to be hoped that making this information readily available will be a memorial to a man who fervently believed in equality and freedom from all forms of slavery

-Ruth Sutherland-
October 1998

My interest in genealogical research began several years ago when my husband and I decided we would try to discover his "roots." He knew that his grandfather had come from McDaniel on the Eastern Shore of Maryland and his grandmother from Accomack on the Eastern Shore of Virginia. The research became a fascinating journey into the history of African Americans in Maryland and Virginia. To our amazement, we were able to discover that his grandmother's family had been free since the late 1600s and his grandfather's since the late 1700s.

Performing this research, I became familiar with the various records at the county courthouses and the Hall of Records in Annapolis. I found that some counties have the unindexed records of the Certificates of Freedom, and a few have the 1832 List of Free Blacks taken for the Colonization Society efforts. More importantly I learned that although there are many records on slaves and free blacks, they are often buried in the land and chattel records, making research time consuming and frustrating.

When I began the research on my own Greenfield family genealogy in Harford County, I discovered my ancestors had also been in Maryland since the late 1600s. I found relatives I didn't know I had, including Elizabeth Black Hoopes. Her grandfather and my great-grandmother were brother and sister. She and her husband, Herbert Hoopes, are Quakers and members at the Little Falls Meeting House in Fallston, Maryland. After learning of my interest in genealogy, they arranged to show me the library at the Meeting House. It was there I found the work of Hunter Sutherland.

# FOREWARD

I had a memory of Mr. Sutherland, as he had been the principal of Bel Air Elementary School when I was there in 1953-1957. In the library files was a folder containing the results of his research with the original wills, land and chattel records of Harford County. In the folder were two typewritten lists, one documenting the manumissions and one documenting the slave sales, each with hundreds of entries.

While reviewing the lists, I saw the entries that made the information represent more than just historical research to me. For, in those lists, I found the names of several of my Greeenfield ancestors, both as sellers and manumitters. Thus, my marriage did truly represent the union of the child of the slave and the child of the slave owner.

Because of the prior research into my husband's family history, I recognized the importance of Mr. Sutherland's data. I knew that it could prove invaluable to African Americans researching their Harford County genealogy. I also believed that it could be valuable for those, like myself, descendants of the slave owners who honestly wanted to learn about their ancestors. Therefore, I felt it needed to be widely available, instead of remaining in a folder in the Meeting House library. I contacted his widow, Ruth Sutherland, who had been a classmate of my mother's at Old Post Road School. I explained my thoughts to her and asked for permission to take her husband's research data and convert it to a format which could be published.

She agreed, and this book is the result.

~Carolyn Greenfield Adams

# INTRODUCTION

## SLAVE MANUMISSIONS

The U.S. Census data show that there was an increasing growth in the ratio of slave to free blacks in Harford County. By the last census before the Civil War in 1860 almost 67% of the blacks were free when compared to less than 20% in 1790. While the total number of blacks, both free and slave, remained relatively constant in the forty years from 1820-1860, the percentage of free blacks more than doubled.

| YEAR | FREE | SLAVE | % FREE |
|------|------|-------|--------|
| 1790 | 775 | 3,417 | 18 |
| 1800 | 1,344 | 4,264 | 24 |
| 1810 | 2,221 | 4,431 | 33 |
| 1820 | 1,367 | 3,320 | 30 |
| 1830 | 2,058 | 2,947 | 41 |
| 1840 | 2,436 | 2,643 | 48 |
| 1850 | 2,777 | 2,166 | 56 |
| 1860 | 3,644 | 1,800 | 67 |

A major factor in this change was the trend in manumissions. The information in this book is based on data from over five hundred documents representing a total of about two thousand of those manumissions.

There were several laws pertaining to the manumission of slaves in Maryland that are reflected in the data. First, in 1752, a law was passed which provided that "persons under land and seal with two witnesses may grant freedom to a slave, if not indebted to creditors and if slave is not over 50 years of age and able to live by work." Then in 1815, a new manumission law was enacted which stated that freedom could " be granted to a slave if under 45 years of age, in good health, able to care for self and earn a living." These laws can be seen reflected in the wording and timing of many of the manumissions.

- In 1817 Sarah Patterson stated that "Negro Sam, under 45 is free as of this date."

- In 1800 Samuel Gover stated "Negro Tony who is able to provide agst. Old age is hereby free."

- In 1822 John Ashmore stated "Fol. Negroes are henceforth free: Samuel, Abraham and Nelly–all under 45, & Nelly's son William–3."

# INTRODUCTION

However, like many of the laws relating to slavery, manumission, and marriage these laws were not fully enforced in Harford County. There were several instances of slaves over the maximum age being manumitted. One example was in 1814 when Henry Stump freed the following slaves: Margaret, age 60, Jack, age 54, along with others under the age of 50. It is possible that provisions for their old age security were made by the owners and not formally recorded, however.

There are several other trends relating to the manumissions in Harford County revealed in the data from these records which give more insight into the rationale and social forces at work in the society at that time. Most significantly, approximately one third of all the manumissions were not immediate. Instead they contained delay clauses that enabled the owners to manumit their slaves, yet still receive a good measure of work and value from them.

These delayed manumissions contained several categories for the delays. One strategy was to manumit the slaves after a specified number of years of service.

- In 1818 James Criswell stated "Negro Winston –14 is to be free after 10 years of service."

- In 1798 Samuel Doherty stated "Free Negroes viz: Bill in 5 yrs.; Rachel in 7 yrs.; Naomi in 16 yrs.; Hagar in 19 yrs.; Rich in 5 yrs.; Sam in 10 yrs.; Dick in 12 yrs.; Sall in 10 yrs.; Dinah and Amy in 12 yrs."

Many of the manumissions granted freedom when the slave or slaves attained a specified age.

- In 1794 Philip Gover stated "slave William, age 12, is to be freed at age of 35."

- In 1830 William Brown stated "To be free at 30: maria-20, Caroline-11, mahala-20 and Delia-3 to be free at 21; any issue of these to be free at 25 if girls, 35 if boys; to be free at 35: Cyrus-16, Henry-9, Sandy-5, Tom-2.

Some contained provisions which covered both a specified time and an age for different slaves, often the children.

- In 1818 William Allen stated that "Negro Julett-16 is to be free in 11 years; Any issue male to be free at 25, female at age 21."

# INTRODUCTION

Others specified that the manumission be upon the death of the owner as in 1860 when Henretta Delmas freed "My Negroes Charles Augustus and Mary Ann and any issue are to be manumitted and set free at my natural death.

The records also indicate that some slaves were freed for philosophical and/or moral. The spirit of the American Revolution and the Declaration of Independence apparently influenced many of these manumissions. Most of these were in the period of the 1770 through the 1790s. The last manumission recorded with this type of comment was in 1804.

- In 1776 Samuel Harris "Being concerned over the injustice of keeping them" freed ten slaves as they reached the age of 25.

- In 1785 William Bond, stated "Freedom is the natural right of mankind" as he freed Harry, age 30.

- In 1786 Joseph Stiles, Innkeeper at Bush stated, 'Slavery is an infringement on the natural rights of man" as he made arrangement for the freedom of six mulattos.

Religion also played a significant role in the rise in manumissions in Harford County. Together the Quakers and the Methodists comprised a significant percentage of the population of the county. During the late 1700s both of these religions took a strong moral stand against slavery. The Quakers developed their philosophy gradually until, by the early 1800s, members were no longer allowed to own slaves. These motives were sometimes stated in the manumissions.

- In 1785 John Lewis freed James with the statement, "holding slaves is repugnant to the laws of God."

- In 1787 Isaac Webster, the Quaker owner of "Broom's Bloom" stated "Laws of God teach all men to do as they would be done unto" as he arranged for the freedom of his slaves as they reached legal age.

The special relationship with the Quakers can be seen in an unusual manumission from Paca Smith of 1830 which stated that "Negro Rachael, age 37, is hereby free. Her children Lydia-7, Mary-5, Charles-3 Cassandra-1 are to be under the control of Joshua Husband. John Jewett, James Cole, Samuel Hopkins, Aquil Massey, David Malsby, Wm. Worthington & John Quarles (Trustees of Deer Creek Friends Meeting) until the girls are 18 and the boys are 21 when each will be free."

# INTRODUCTION

The Methodists also originally banned members from owning slaves. However they gradually changed their position to that of a ban on deacons or preachers purchasing slaves and mandating that a newly purchased slave must be given a manumission date as terms of the purchase. This is probably reflected in the number of sales with delayed manumission terms.

The gender of the owner also appears to have played a significant role in the manumission transactions. Approximately twenty-six percent of all the manumissions were executed by female owners. This figure is twice as high as the percentage of sellers or buyers of slaves who were female.

Of those that were manumitted, about five percent were near the end of their productive years, over the age of 40, and thus nearing the age at which manumitting them would no longer have been legal. Another five percent were between thirty-five and forty years old.

- In 1803 Jacob Forwood stated "Negro Nance, age 43, is hereby free."

- In 1825 Jacob Giles stated "Negro Samuel-43 is to be free on 1/1/1827."

Several of the manumissions reflected the end process of the slave purchasing their own freedom as evidenced by a statement "on payment" or "in consideration" of a sum of money. Many more of the manumissions could have resulted from such arrangements, but were not officially recorded as such.

- In 1809 Ruth Willmott - "On paym't of $100, Negro Harry is henceforth free."

- In 1822 Wm. Wilson, et al "In con. of $100, Negro Andrew Bond is hereby set free."

The records also show that although some slaves were manumitted, this did not free them from negotiated appreticeships. One example was in 1795 when Charles Worthington stated "Negro Harry and his children: Sarah, Mary, Hannah, David, John, Margaret, Charles, Sharper and Caesar are hereby free; however freedom is not to interfere with apprentices."

# INTRODUCTION

Especially interesting is the fact that approximately three percent of the manumissions recorded were to free blacks who purchased the slaves, usually relatives, to free them.

- In 1790, Edward Hopkins, colored, "For natural love and affection that I bear my son whom I purchased from Richard Robinson."

- In 1798 Negro Jack freed Negro woman Fanny, age 32, bought from Benj. Everett and then listed five children by name to be freed upon reaching legal age- 21 for males and 16 for females.

- In 1810 Adams Bond, Negro purchased from Mary Bond Estate and set free his wife Hannah and children Bill, Jonathan, Levy and Mary Ann.

- In 1815 John Durbin, free black, "For natural love and affection for my children, all males to be free at 21, females at 16; Stephen, Grace, Mary, Hannah, Harret, Susan, Isabella, Bonaparte, Elizabeth, Christian and Bennett.

- In 1815 Chas Williams, "My yellow woman, Mary, being my wife and her 3 ch. are free."

The final manumissions came as a result of the Civil War, when the male slaves who enlisted in a Colored Regiment of the Union Army were set free and the master compensated. Forty-three men who gained their freedom in this manner in Harford County. Ten in 1863, thirty in 1864 and three in 1865. The last was on August 31, 1865. From the National American:

February 26, 1864.
In this month is the first advance for recruiting "Colored Troops". They are to be between the ages of 18 and 45, males. If free, each is to get $300 bounty from the state; those of Baltimore City $500. A slave is to get a bounty of $100 from the state, the master the same amount and if loyal, $300 from the United States."

March 18, 1864
Another draft has been ordered calling for 200,000 men in addition to the 500,000 ordered for February. Volunteers are to be received until April 15, when drafting will begin if necessary- bounty $100.

May 13, 1864
Quota for Harford County in the draft which takes place today is 323 men.

# INTRODUCTION

Historians have noted trends in overall manumissions in Maryland that show individuals who manumitted a slave or slaves would also later purchase others. This does not appear to have occurred often in Harford County. Of those individuals who manumitted a slave or slaves only approximately three percent later bought any other slaves. In several instances those slaves manumitted were of an advanced age, several were over 45. One example of this was in 1807 when George Chauncy manumitted Negroes Simon-60, Cato-70 and Rose-70. In 1819 he bought Negroes Stokes-43 and Stansbury-16 for $500.00.

However, about ten percent of those owners who manumitted slaves then also sold a slave or slaves, often to other family members. Almost half of these sales contained provisions for the later manumission of the slave(s). An example is when in 1821 Ady Chloe sold to her daughter Ady for 5 shillings a Negro girl Sarah-6 " to serve until the age of 34."

## SLAVE SALES

The records of slave sales also contained some interesting trends. The most obvious is that the selling of slaves was a very local business. Approximately ninety percent of the sales were transacted between local citizens of Harford County and many were to relatives.

- In 1784 Josiah Hichcock sold to Randall Hichcock "Negroes: Hannah-26, Graw-20, Dinah & Phobe-2 and Lydia, 6 months."

- In 1794 "John Hay of Joppa" sold to "Son, John Hay and Dau, Margaret Hay" Negroes Sharper, James, Perry, Sal and Judah for the price of "love & aff. And 5 shillings."

Only during the period 1818 through 1839 there was a trend to sell to out of state buyers when about eighteen percent of all sales during the period were to these out of state buyers. One of the most infamous was Austin Woolfolk who maintained a slave action in Baltimore City from which the slaves were generally sold South. Other buyers included John Nolan of Georgia, John Nichols and James Menefee both of Tennessee. The prices to these buyers were generally higher than those to the local buyers, but it could have been that they tended to purchase prime field hands or slaves with specific skills whose values were higher.

# INTRODUCTION

The effect of the age restrictions of the manumission laws can also be seen in the sales records. In 1852 Robert Holland sold Mary Christy to Charles Christy-colored - for the price of $1.00, as she "cannot be manumitted as she is over 45 years of age."

Female sellers or buyers amounted to only thirteen percent of the total sales transactions as compared with twenty-six percent of the manumissions. Of these sales fully thirty-nine percent were to other family members and many times there was no money involved in the transaction. One example of this is when in 1779 Ann Amos sold to Susannah Amos for the price of "love and affection" one Negro girl Jane.

The records clearly show how the slaves were often sold along with other goods often as a result of the death of the owner and inventory of his possessions. Approximately thirteen percent of all the sales fell into this category. These types of sales were most common during the period of the 1790s through early 1800s.

- In 1786 for 85:18:03 Archibald Smithson sold to John Orrick of Baltimore County "Negro girls: Bet & Hannah; Negro boy Tom, and one bay horse called 'Bloody Buttocks'."

- In 1788 for 150 pounds Wm. Fell Day sold to John Fulton a silver watch, Negro Phebe and her 4 children, 3 horses, 4 cows etc.

- In 1799 Benj. Smithson sold to Dorsey Howard one stud horses, 2 cows, one sow & 7 pigs, one yellow girl, 2 beds, case drawers, spinning wheel etc.

Usually a woman and her small children were sold together, but not always.

- In 1778 Josiah Hichcock sold to Isaac Montgomery for 69 pounds one Negro girl, Meriah, age 14 ms and to James Pocock he sold for 100 ponds Negro girl Ruth, age 8 mos.

- In 1801 Frances Mitchell for 93:15:00 sold to Bennett Wheeler one Negro girl Rachael, age 9, one boy Joe, age 6 and one sorrel mare.

Occasionally slaves were sold by the sheriff for taxes as in 1794 when John Bond, Sheriff, sold Negro Limus to Joseph Strong for 3:16:09.

# INTRODUCTION

Another interesting transaction occurred in 1827 when Wm. Shell sold the Negro Jacob "who is now absounded and run away" to Barnett Billingslea for $150. Mr. Billingslea must have thought there was a good chance of finding Jacob to have invested $150 in the speculative purchase.

The sales could also be combined with a delayed manumission. Overall about ten percent of the slaves were sold for a limited period of time then to be manumitted, again perhaps reflecting the influence of the Methodists.

- In 1831 Negro Abraham sold for $200 until 1838 "when he is to be set free."

- In 1807 Joseph Ford sold to Joshua fFrd his brother for 5 shillings "Negroes Isaac and Darkey for life; son John to serve until 21 and then to be manumitted; also Abagail to serve 6 years, Teany for 7 years., Sophia for 16 yrs., Solomon for 21 yrs., and Henry for 23 yrs., thereafter each is to be manumitted and set free.

Sometimes free Negroes bought slaves. Approximately four percent of the sales were to free Negroes who usually bought their relatives so they could then free them.

- In 1794 Negro Pompey, late servant of Wm. Hopkins, pur. Negro Sarah & her 2 children for 17 pounds.

- In 1831 Otho Scott sold to harry Preston, a Black man, Negro Caroline, 16 and her 2 children.

- In 1836 Harry Preston, Col, presented to his niece Colored Caroline Stephenson, one colored lad America, son of Caroline.

- In 1833 Margaret Denneson, free woman of color, pd $30 for John Denneson, her husband.

There is one sale in 1848 that is particularly interesting because "Corbin Bond, free man of color" paid "John McKenney of Washington D.C. a penny for one Negro child, Sarah Jane, age 8, Corbin Bond's daughter." This showed that he knew that his daughter was owned by a resident of Washington D.C. and that he was allowed to purchase her for a penny.

# INTRODUCTION

The prices varied greatly during any period. American money was first used as exchange in 1796 when Edward Prall sold a Negro woman Nan and girls Lily and Judy to James Thompson for $38.00. It was interesting to note that English money was used primarily until the War of 1812. The last sale using English values was recorded in 1814 and was for 5 shillings and debt payment.

## NAMES

Most genealogical researchers are interested in the derivation of the slave surnames. It is a commonly held belief that slaves often took the surnames of their masters. The data for Harford County doesn't lend itself to support this idea directly. Of the one hundred and ninety-four of the slaves sold or manumitted that did have surnames, approximately thirty seven percent had a surname that matched that of a slave holder in the county. However, there was no direct correlation between any of these slave surnames and that of his/her owner at the time of the sale or manumission.

Many of these surnames were such common ones as Brown, Jones, Johnson, Harris or Williams. Such common names would make linking them to a slave owner of the same name unlikely. Yet there were several slave surnames unique enough to surmise that they were taken from those of Harford County slave owners. Those included Billingslea, Bond, Gilbert, Giles, Kell, Lee, Paca, Preston, Rigby and Webster. But even these names were not associated with a slave belonging to them at the time of the manumission or sale. Apparently, the slave surnames originated in prior generations which may have had a more direct connection with that family, or they were chosen by the slaves based on other factors.

The first names of the slaves reflected several naming patterns. Many names were Biblical in origin. Masters may have bestowed these names initially on slaves who then passed them on to following generations. Or the slaves may have chosen these names because of their familiarity with Biblical stories. Moses who led the exodus from Egypt, or Daniel, who survived the lion's den, may have had special significance for a slave. Other popular examples of Biblical names include Abraham, Hagar, Hannah, Isaac, Jacob, James, John, Joshua, Sarah, Solomon, Rachael and Peter.

# INTRODUCTION

A few such as Cato, Ceasar, Chloe, Hercules, Nero and Pompey were probably given by white masters who had studied the classics. There were several that may have retained African origins. These included Mint, Phyllis, Mingo and Olinah.

A few were apparently, the surnames of slave owners such as Merryman, and Stansbury. The slave Hampton apparently bore the name of the Ridgely estate. These names may have been used to identify slaves that had been purchased at one time from those individuals or estates.

# SLAVE MANUMISSIONS

# SLAVE MANUMISSIONS

| Date | Last Name | First Name | Transaction |
|------|-----------|------------|-------------|
| 1775 | Sheridine | Cassandra | To be free at age of 18: Pris and Charlot; Lads to be freed at age of 21; Nacy, Stephen, Jacob, Abrham, Sam, Henry, Plato and Isam. |
| 1776 | Harris | Samuel | "Being concerned over the injustice of keeping them free as they reach 25" free when they reach 25-Fanny, Tober, Rachael, Venee, Lidia, Polly. Free 1/1/1782 -Dinah, Tower. |
| 1778 | Chew | Susannah | Free India and Holiday on 7/1/78 - Free their children when 2. |
| 1778 | Chew | Thomas | Negroes Susanna, George, Sarah are hereby free. |
| 1780 | Debruler | Micajah | Free Negro Ben as of this date. |
| 1780 | Gover | Elizabeth | Free Negoes Sim and Nan as of this date. |
| 1780 | Preston | Clemency | Free boys when 21: Aquila-10, Elijah-8, and Bobin-4; free the girls when 18: Phllis-14, Hannah-5 and Deliah-3. |
| 1781 | Richardson | Hannah | Following free as of this date: Nelly-22, Harry-30. |
| 1782 | Kitely | Rachael | Negroes Darew and Pegg are hereby free; Robert to be free in 10 yrs, Isaac in 20 yrs and Zane in 9 yrs from this date. |
| 1782 | Stanford | Aquila | Negro women Abagail and Rose are hereby freed, their 7 child to be free when boys reach age of 27 and girls 25. |
| 1782 | Presbury | Mary | Negro Lydia and her offspring Pippin to be free 31/1/1782. |
| 1782 | Kell | Thomas | Six Negroes to be freed at various dates from 1783-1793. |
| 1782 | Preston | Bernard | Negoes to be free as foll; Prudence on 10/22/1782, Darby on 4/7/83, Benjamin when 25 yrs old. |
| 1783 | Garrettson | Freeborn | Free Negro James-19 when 21 yrs old. |

1

# SLAVE MANUMISSIONS

| Date | Last Name | First Name | Transaction |
|------|-----------|------------|-------------|
| 1783 | Lee | James | Free male slaves at 21 and girl slaves at 16 as fol: Hagar-1788, Patience'92, Grace '94, Phyllis '96, Tuckey 1797, Pompey '98, Nance '98, Tom '99, Fan 1800 and Simon when he is 30 years old. |
| 1783 | Paca | Aquila | Bequethed in his will to Dr. James Lee who was his maternal grandfather, 16 Negro slaves for purposes of manumission. |
| 1783 | Ruff | Henry | Negro Tom-30 to be free 1/4/1787. |
| 1784 | Lyon | John | Negro Sam is free as of this date. |
| 1784 | Gilbert | Mary | Negroe Thomas to be free as of this date. |
| 1784 | Watters | Henry | Nine Negores to be free at various times up to 1796. |
| 1784 | Dutton | Nann | Negroes Brsto-40 and Tamer-21 are hereby free, the following boy slaves to be free at 21: George, Phil and James. |
| 1784 | Wallis | Joseph | Negro Cleasant Talbutt free as of this date. |
| 1784 | Watters | Henry | 9 Negroes to be free at various times up to 1786. |
| 1785 | Bond | William | "Freedom is the natural right of mankind"; Negro man Harry-30 is hereby free. |
| 1785 | Lewis | John | "Holding slaves is repugnant to the laws of God", Negro James is free as of this date. |
| 1785 | West | Susanna | Negro woman Sarah-22 is hereby free; seven slave children are to be freed when males reach 21 and females 18. |
| 1785 | Wallis | Maragaret | Negro Caesar is to be free with any property acquired as of now. |
| 1785 | West | Susanne | Negro woman Sarah-22, is hereby free; 7 slave children are to be freed when males reach 21 and females 18. |

# SLAVE MANUMISSIONS

| Date | Last Name | First Name | Transaction |
|------|-----------|------------|-------------|
| 1786 | Coleman | Jon | Negroes to be free on Christmas Day as follows:Arthur,1794, David in 1798, James and Fanny in 1805. |
| 1786 | Stiles | Joseph | "Slavery is an infrengement of the natural rights of man", Free on Jan 1 slaves as follows: Diana-1798, Mulatto Bill-1801, Mulatto Jim-1804, Mulatto Isaac-1806,Mulatto Rachael-1806 and Mulatto Joshua-1813. |
| 1786 | Coleman | John | Negroes to be free on Christmas day as follows: Arthur-23, 1794, David-1798, James and Fanny-1805. |
| 1787 | Webster | Isaac | "The law of God teaches all men to do as they would be done unto". Two Negro boys are to be free in 1796; three girls are to be free as they become 18 years of age. |
| 1787 | Wilson | John | Negro women Fortune and Hannah are hereby free; their 9 children are to be free as they become 18 years of age. |
| 1787 | Wilson | Jno & Jos | Negro Tom -36 is hereby free (formerly of Samll Wilson, decd). |
| 1787 | Wilson | Sarah | Negro Luch-13 to be free at age of 18. |
| 1787 | Dallam | Richard | Negroes to be free as foll: Thomas and Peter in 7 yrs, Caesar in 6 yr, Cato in 9 yrs, Yellow Shins in 12 yrs, Joe in 15 yrs, Ned in 20 yrs, Nancy in 14 yrs, and Elinimia in 16 yrs. |
| 1787 | Wilson | Martha | Negro Sarah-32 is hereby free; Will & James to be free at 21. |
| 1787 | Dallam | John | Negro Tom is free as of this date. |
| 1787 | Carroll | Elizabeth | Negroes Joseph and Hannah to be free 10 years from this date. |
| 1787 | Parsons | Daniel | Foll: slaves to be free at age 21; Nathan-3 and Sarah-6 Any offspring by Sarah are to be free at birth. |

# SLAVE MANUMISSIONS

| Date | Last Name | First Name | Transaction |
|------|-----------|------------|-------------|
| 1787 | Lee | Elizabeth | Widow of James Lee -Free Negro girls Lydia in 1797 and Nancy in 1800. Free Boys Duke-1799, Chas 1799, George-1801, Forester 1801. |
| 1787 | Lee | Elizabeth | Free Negro girls: Lydia in 1797, Nancy in 1800, free boys: 1799, Charles-1799, George 1801 and Forrest 1801. |
| 1787 | Dallam | John | Negro Tom age 36 is free as of this date. |
| 1787 | Carroll | Elizabeth | Negroes Joseph and Hannah to be freed 10 years from this date. |
| 1787 | McGowan | Capt Jno | For Rachael Nevill -Negroes Nan and Sam are hereby free as of this date. |
| 1788 | Hopkins | Joseph | Negro woman Cumbo is free as of this date. |
| 1788 | Webster | Joseph | Negro Tony is free as of this date. |
| 1789 | Dallam | Richard | Negro James is free as of this date. |
| 1789 | Robertson | Daniel | Free Negro girls: Jenny, Nell, Nan and any offspring when 18; free boys: Jack & Mingo with any property acq at 21. |
| 1789 | Wilson | Samuel | "to all Christian people", Negro London is to be freed after seven years of services. |
| 1790 | Hanson | Elizabeth | Negro Sarah is to be free July next; Charlotte 10 yrs fr.now. |
| 1790 | Hopkins-Colored | Edward | "For natural love and affection that I bear my son whom I purch. From Richard Robinson" to be free on Aug 28, 1790. |
| 1791 | Baker | Charles | For nine pounds specie paid by Edward Howard Freeman for the Negro woman Theba is hereby free. |
| 1791 | Mathers | Michael | Negro boy Jacob-12 is to be freed when 25 years of age. |
| 1791 | Massey | Aquilla | Negro woman Tamer is hereby free; boy Jim to be freed at 25. |

4

# SLAVE MANUMISSIONS

| Date | Last Name | First Name | Transaction |
|------|-----------|------------|-------------|
| 1791 | Webster | Samuel | Negro Samuel Webster(?) is hereby free. |
| 1792 | Lytle | Ann | Negro Ester-30 and one year old child henceforth free. |
| 1792 | McCan | David | Negro Nance recently sold to me by Sam'l Scott is hereby free. |
| 1792 | White | Steven | 3 year apprentice smith to Steven White, blacksmith. |
| 1792 | Hall | Sabina | Negro woman Margaret-30 is hereby free. |
| 1792 | Jones | Stephen | Negro Phyllis is hereby freed 14 years from this date. |
| 1792 | Horne | Nicholas | Negro Fanny age 42 is hereby free. |
| 1792 | Bond | Jacob | Negro Dinah wife of Dick freed by John Dutton is free. |
| 1792 | Wilson of Jos. | John | 9 children of freed Negroes Fortune and Hannah are to be free when boys are 21 , girls 18: Joshua, Sophia, Comfort, Deliah,Dolly,Jenny, Linda, Lucky,  Milky. |
| 1792 | Bond | James | Negroes Cato-46 and Will-37 are hereby free. |
| 1793 | Archer | John | Executor for Moses Rath; Negro Sam, Rott, Rachaelt and Stephen are to be freed at age of 31 years. |
| 1793 | Wilson | Joseph | Negro Ned, age about 40, is hereby free. |
| 1793 | Dallam | John | Negro Nellie is hereby free;her daughters Grace-4 yrs 8 mo and Rose 1 yr 8 mo to be free at age of 18. |
| 1793 | Carlile | Lancelot | Negro man Mannus is henceforth free. |
| 1793 | Archer | John | Negro Joe, negro Prima and wife Dina are hereby free. |
| 1793 | Street | John | Negro Sam, age 21, is hereby free. |

# SLAVE MANUMISSIONS

| Date | Last Name | First Name | Transaction |
|------|-----------|------------|-------------|
| 1793 | Smithson | William | Negro Sam, age 21, is hereby free 1805; Jack in 1806. |
| 1793 | Osborn | Benjamin | Negro Combo, age 34, is hereby free; Hannah-15, Polly-14, and Priss-4, to be free at 21; Harry-2, to be free at 26. |
| 1793 | McMath | William | Negro Rose, age 42, is hereby free. |
| 1793 | Howard | Lemuel | Negroes Guinea and Samuel, each about 49, are to be free next Christmas Day. |
| 1793 | Dutton | John | Suck. Age 47, and Nan, age 46, slaves for life, are free. |
| 1793 | Cromwell | Venisha | Negro Pero is to be free 8 years, 6 months from this date. |
| 1794 | York | Mary | Negro Abraham is to be free at age 25. |
| 1794 | Greenfield | Jacob | Negroes Joe and Hannah are freed as of this date. |
| 1794 | Baine | Samuel | "Mulotto" women Mararet, age 30, is free as of this date. |
| 1794 | Garrettson | George | Negro Tom, age 33, is to be free on Dec. 22, 1794. |
| 1794 | Gover | Philip | Slave William, age 12, is to be freed at age of 35. |
| 1794 | Hill | George | Nego Esthe, 51, is hereby free; Boy John, 11, free at 2; Girls Molly-13, and Ann, 8, to be free at 16. |
| 1794 | Holland | Francis | Negro George & wife Margaret; Negro William Guin and wife Violet are henceforth free. |
| 1794 | Whiteford | Hugh | Negro Prissilla- 18 is free at age 28. |
| 1794 | Worthington | John | Negroes David- 45, Cesar- 35, Jenny-40, Fanny- 40, Desen-29, Hector-20, are hereby freed; Lidid-21, and Tower-16 are to be free at age 26. |

# SLAVE MANUMISSIONS

| Date | Last Name | First Name | Transaction |
|------|-----------|------------|-------------|
| 1794 | Wright | Thomas | Female child Alice, age 18 mos. is hereby free. |
| 1794 | Steal | Wm. & Marg't | Negroe Harriet-7, and Julia 4 are to be free at age 21. |
| 1794 | Ruff | Henry | Negro Thomas-18, to be free in 1801; Ned-12, as of 1807. |
| 1794 | Mather | Michael | Negro Lundon, age 23, is to be fee Christmas next. |
| 1794 | Luckie | William | Negro Peter, age 33, is free as of this date. |
| 1794 | Mather | Joanne | Negro girl Clo, age 15, is to be free at age 25. |
| 1794 | Bryarly | Robert | Negro Lenn is free henceforth. |
| 1795 | Morris | Israel | Negro Charles and wife Pug are hereby free; Free children when boys 21, girls 18: Howard, Aquila, Milcha, Hannah, Maria, Sophia, Charles. |
| 1795 | Worthington | Charles | Negro Harry and his children: Sarah, Mary, Hannah, David, John, Margaret, Charles, Sharper, and Caesar are hereby free; however freedoom is not to interfere with apprentices. |
| 1795 | Moore | Daniel | Harry-15, age 15, is to be free at the age of 31 in 1811. |
| 1795 | Abbott | David | Negroes Phoebe and her children: Frances, Benn, Trush, Freeborn, and San are hereby free. |
| 1796 | Everist | Joseph | Negro Brazil is hereby free. |
| 1796 | Peck | Samuel | Negro Poll is hereby free. |
| 1796 | Cox | Israel | Free as follows: Andrew as of now; Lucy on 1/1/1798; Simon, on 1/1/1807; James on 2/15/1814; Jane on 1/1/1807 and Free by 4/15/1813. |

7

# SLAVE MANUMISSIONS

| Date | Last Name | First Name | Transaction |
|------|-----------|------------|-------------|
| 1796 | Dallam | Josias | Negro Harry, bought at Sherriff's sale from Winston Smith, is hereby free. |
| 1796 | Carroll | Benjamin | Negroes Sarah-38, Georg-24, and Harry-18 are hereby free. |
| 1796 | Carroll | Ann | Roy Valentine, age 4, is to be free at age of 35; Slave women Ismeah is to be free at my death. |
| 1796 | Gallup | Joseph | Negro girl Harriot is to be free on Aug. 7, 1815. |
| 1797 | Bond | John | Mulatto Sam, age 38, is hereby free. |
| 1797 | Worthington | Charles | Negroes Tower and Nanny are hereby free; Harry, son of Harry, sold to Timpleton & Co. for 7 yrs.m is free on 1/23/1805. |
| 1797 | McComas | William | Negro Sampson and wife Jane are herby free. |
| 1797 | Gower | Philip | "Molato" girl Darker-12 is to be free at age of 33; Negro George-9 is to be free at age 35. |
| 1798 | Johnson | William | Mulatto Sam is hereby free. |
| 1798 | Moores | John | Negro Jack age 43 is hereby free. |
| 1798 | Bond | Jacob | Negro Sam-40, Murror-40, Hannah 39 are hereby free. |
| 1798 | Dougherty | Samuel | Free Negroes viz:Bill in 5 years, Rachael in 7 yrs, Naomi in 16 yrs., Hagar in 19 yrs., Rich in 5 years, Sam in 10 yrs., Dick in 12 yrs.,Sal in 10 years, Diah and Amy in 12 years. |
| 1798 | | Negro Jack | Negro Fanny age 32 bought from Benjamin Everett, is hereby free. Freeborn-11,Ned-9, Jack-7, Jim-5 are to be free at age 21; Negro Milla age 2 is to be free at age 16. |
| 1798 | Johnson | James | Negro Nan-24, is hereby free; her girl Caroline- 17 months is to be free on 12/1/1817 but any issue is to slave until free. |

8

# SLAVE MANUMISSIONS

| Date | Last Name | First Name | Transaction |
|------|-----------|------------|-------------|
| 1798 | Mather | Michael | Negro Peter, age 20, living with Frances Holland, Esq., is to be free at age 30; Tony, age 38, is to be free in 5 years;Becky, age 19, is to be free at age of 38 and any issue to be free at age of 25. |
| 1799 | Dougherty | Samuel | Negro Dick now in Thornberry PA is hereby free. |
| 1799 | Dallam | Josias | Negro Frank,42, is hereby free. |
| 1799 | Madow | John | Negro Sam,36, and Abagail,36, are hereby free. |
| 1799 | Milligan | James | "Black Garill Paul" is hereby free. |
| 1799 | Wilson | William | Negro Dearo alias Nadira is to be free in seven years. |
| 1800 | Mitchell | Thomas | As of this date the following are free: two mulatto boys, Mitchel and Jonas; also Negro Vera Margaret. |
| 1800 | Luckie | John | "Being conscientiously scrupulous of hooping[sic]slaves" Negro Martin age 10 is to be free at age 28. |
| 1800 | Giles | JoAnn | Following Negroes are hereby free: Susan, Milk, Will, Lidia; Paraway-9, to be free at age 26;Ann-13, to be free at 20. |
| 1800 | Gover | Samuel | Negro Tony is able to provide agst. old age is hereby free. |
| 1800 | Hill- Negro | Tower | Elizabeth my wife and daughter purchased from Edward C. Tolby are hereby free. |
| 1800 | Rumsey | Benjamin | Negro Santi and Mulatto Bridgit are hereby free. |
| 1800 | Ward | Richard | Negro boys Mose and Jess are to be free at age 21. |
| 1800 | Wilmott | Ruth | William, lately served seven years to Thomas Thompson in Kentucky is hereby free. |

# SLAVE MANUMISSIONS

| Date | Last  Name | First Name | Transaction |
|------|-----------|------------|-------------|
| 1801 | Watters | Stephen | One Negro woman to be free in six years; two children are to be free at age 25. |
| 1801 | Smith | Jacob Giles | Negro Batts is free as of this date. |
| 1801 | Renshaw | Joseph | Negro James is to be free three years from this date. |
| 1801 | Horner | Nicholas | Free the following Negroes at age 25: Samson-23, Beck-20, Fan-11, Stephen-3, Sidi-1 and Isaac-5. |
| 1801 | Crawford | Leabon | Negro Moses is to be free on Oct 10, 1802. |
| 1802 | Giles | JoAnna | Negro George is hereby free; Amy-13, to be free at 25; Negro Parawasy-10 is to be free at age of 31. |
| 1802 | Gover | Robert | Negro Murier is hereby free. |
| 1802 | Jarrett | Bennett | Mulatto Ned, 24 is to free on 3/1/1814. |
| 1802 | Smith | Paca | "I give little girl Polly to Isaac, her father; Isaac Washington frees Polly as of this date." |
| 1802 | Forwood | Jacob | Negro Nance age 43 is hereby free. |
| 1803 | Bond | Buckler | Negro Nathan age 43 is hereby free. |
| 1803 | Dallam | William | Negro Benjamin, the bearer is a free man. |
| 1803 | Gover | Priscilla | Negro Hannah is free on this date; Sam to be free in May 1810 and William in March 1813. |
| 1803 | Coale | Samuel | "Negro Belinda was freed by certif. To quakers in 1799 at the age of 18.  This document is now clear and legal." |
| 1804 | Bankhead | William | Negro Bash is to be free at end of two years service. |
| 1804 | Hall | Jonas | Following are released from slavery: Sharper-44, Diamond and his woman Hannah. |

# SLAVE MANUMISSIONS

| Date | Last Name | First Name | Transaction |
|------|-----------|------------|-------------|
| 1804 | Hayes | Ester | Negro Sal age 43 is hereby free. |
| 1804 | Norris | Elizabeth | Black woman Ann, called Nan, is hereby free. |
| 1804 | Smith | Jacob Gile | Jacob Roberts, Easter and Betsy Roberts daughters of Orange Roberts, are hereby free. |
| 1804 | Stump | Elizabeth | "Believe in freedom to be the inaliable right of all human beings, I set free the following slaves: Negro Cesar-22, Sukey-25, and Deliah-18 months." |
| 1804 | Webster, Sr. | Samuel | Negro Minty-22 is hereby freed. |
| 1804 | Wilson | William | Negro Betty-30 and her child Letty-2 is hereby free. Negro Phyllis is to be free at age of 28. |
| 1804 | Worthington | William | Negro Girl Ann-7 is to be free on 1/1/1825 when the sale to James Johnson expires. |
| 1804 | Barnes-heir | Elizabeth | "Conceiving it her natural right and consonant to the verbal testamony of her mistress, Negro Rachael, 42, is hereby free. |
| 1805 | Trapnell | Rebecca | Negro woman Rachael and Thebe, hired by my late father for 15 years in 1804, are to be free at the end of this obligation. |
| 1805 | Dallam | Richard | Negro Sarah-25 and son Harry 15 days are hereby free. |
| 1805 | Trapnell | Rebecca | Following Slaves are to be free at the age of 28: Elizabeth, Martha, Amelia, Elenor, Pender, Sophia, Susan, Sidney, Dalia, Belinda- any issue to be free at age 28; Also, free at 28: Stephen, Edward, Abraham, Joseph, George. |
| 1805 | Hall | Elizabeth | Negro Tom age 40 is hereby free. |
| 1805 | Hall | John | Negro Bell-14 is to be free in 12 years along with any property that she may acquire. |

11

# SLAVE MANUMISSIONS

| Date | Last Name | First Name | Transaction |
|------|-----------|------------|-------------|
| 1805 | McMath | William | Negro girl Charlotte, age 16 sold to Zero Hughes until 1/16/1817 is to become free on that date. |
| 1806 | Cowan | Elenor | Following are free as of this date: Negro Nancy-4, and her children: Alexander-4 and Henry-1. |
| 1806 | Evitt | Margaret | Negro girls Dorcas-14 and Nancy-12 are freed "so they might bind themselves to me as servants until they are 28." |
| 1806 | Monks | Richard | Negro Charles, age 20, is hereby free on Jan. 1, 1817. |
| 1806 | Osborn | John | One hundred dollars paid, Negro Jim is henceforth free. |
| 1806 | Wilmott | Ruth | Negro women Eleanor-31, is hereby free and her Children: Rachel and Elizabeth are to be free at the age of 20. |
| 1807 | Hopkins | Charles | Negro Joe is free as of this date. |
| 1807 | Yellott | John | Negro Hagar, age 41, is henceforth free. |
| 1807 | Worthington, et al | Joe | Negro man Caesar is henceforth free. |
| 1807 | Rigdon | Stephen | Negro women Nanney, wife of Thos. Newitt, and children: North-13, Lebina-7, and Stephen 4 are hereby free. |
| 1807 | Kenly | Richard | Negro George, age 38, is henceforth free. |
| 1807 | Hopkins | Samuel | Negro Jacob Jones, age 44, is henceforth free. |
| 1807 | Guest-Philadelphia | John | Following slaves are hereby free: Hannah, age 40, Rachel, age 25, Richard-7, and William-5. |
| 1807 | Davis | John | Jane is to become free upon the decease of John Davis & wife; Bets to be free 1 yr. Later, Cato 5 yrs. Later, Bobb 11 yrs. Later, Tom 15 yrs. Later, Juliet 15 yrs. Later, and Labine 17 yrs. later. |

# SLAVE MANUMISSIONS

| Date | Last Name | First Name | Transaction |
|------|-----------|------------|-------------|
| 1807 | Creswell | Mary | Negro women Rachel, age 35, is henceforth free. |
| 1807 | Coleman | John | Freedom of 1785 invalidated by lack of witnesses; Arther and David are henceforth free. |
| 1807 | Chauncy | Georg | Negroes Simon-60, Cato-70, and Rose 70 are henceforth free. |
| 1807 | Hanson | John | Negro Moses Maringo, age 42, is henceforth free. |
| 1807 | Howard | Leonard | Negro Isaac, age 35, is henceforth free. |
| 1808 | Hall | William | Following slaves are to be free after 10 years of faithful service: George-21, Peter-24, Jonas-20, Dinah- 19. |
| 1808 | Wilson | William | Negroes David and Lusanna are henceforth free. |
| 1808 | Parsons | Caleb | My son Moses Parsons, purchased from Rob't Creswell, is free. |
| 1808 | Prigg | Edward | 40 pounds pd. By Hamilton Morgan, Negro Tisshe is to be free in 6 years; Any issue, if male free at 21, female-20. |
| 1809 | Carrol | James | Negro girl Sarah, age 10, to be free at age of 25. |
| 1809 | Wright | John | Negro Peter, age 26, is henceforth free. |
| 1809 | Wilmott | Ruth | On paym't of $100. Negro Harry is henceforth free. |
| 1809 | Sexton | Elizabet | Following slaves are free as each reaches age of 38: Andrew-31, David-26, Grace-28, Amy-13, and Margaret-9. |
| 1809 | Watters | Godfrey | Negro Jacob, age 26, is hereby free. |
| 1809 | Hopkins | Samuel | Negro Hannah, age 40, is henceforth free. |
| 1809 | Dadford | Benjamin | Negro Thomas, age 10, is henceforth free. |

# SLAVE MANUMISSIONS

| Date | Last Name | First Name | Transaction |
|------|-----------|------------|-------------|
| 1809 | Bond | John | Negro Elijah, son of Poll, age 2, is to be free at age 21. |
| 1809 | Bolster | William | Negro Samson is henceforth free. |
| 1809 | Webster | Samuel | Negro man Isaac, age 27, is henceforth free. |
| 1809 | Preston | Aquil | Negro Abraham, age 43, is hereby free. |
| 1810 | Kennard | Isaac | Negro girl Easter, age 26, is hereby free on this day. |
| 1810 | Cain | Elizabeth | Negro women Nancy is to be free on June 1, 1821. |
| 1810 | Webster | Samuel | Negro Jack. Age 35, is hereby free. |
| 1810 | Wilson | Peter | Negro Cumberland, age 21, is hereby free. |
| 1810 | Webster | John S. | Negro Patience & her daughter Sulky-2, are hereby freed. |
| 1810 | Stump | William | Negro Hannah, 28, is hereby free; her Children to be free- girls at age 18, boys at age 21- Betty-13, Jane-8, Charles-3, and Molly-1. |
| 1810 | Prigg | Edward | Negro women Milkey, age 27, and infant Thomas are hereby free. |
| 1810 | Dutton | John | Following Negroes are henceforth free: Candice-35, Pris-18, Betty-16, Radner-14, Davy-14, and Mary-17. |
| 1810 | Dulaney | Joshua | Negroes to be free on Following dates: Margaret-37, in 1815; Hariet-8, in 1828; Patience-6. In 1830; Prince-4, in 1832 ; Ben-3mos. In 1838- all to be freed on August 1. |
| 1810 | Chocks (Cholck) | Tudor | Negro Grace, 43, is hereby free; Grace's daughter Mary, age 3, is to serve Richard Culane un'til 18 and then to be free. |

# SLAVE MANUMISSIONS

| Date | Last Name | First Name | Transaction |
|------|-----------|------------|-------------|
| 1810 | Bond | Dennis | Adam Bond, Negro, purchased from Mary Bond, Estate, and set free his wife Hannah and Children Bill, Jonathan Levy, and Mary Ann. |
| 1810 | Rumsey | John | As Exec. Of Benj. Rumsey's will, Negro Joe, age 34, is hereby and henceforth free. |
| 1811 | Morgan | Robert | Negro women Margate-23 is hereby free; Bet-30, to be free on 12 / 1 / 1811 and her ch. When 21, viz: Harriet-13, Very-9; Hannah-4. |
| 1811 | McMath | William | Negro George, age 40, is henceforth free. |
| 1811 | Turnpaugh | John | Negro Bill-13 is to be free when 35 yrs. old. |
| 1811 | Ruth- Free Negro | Samuel | My daughter, Hasnnah, is hereby freed, at 10 mos. of age, but she is to stay with Tudor Cholck until she is 16. |
| 1811 | Husband | Rachel | Negro Dinah is hereby freed on Dec. 1, 1813 when 20 yrs. old; her children: Betty Husband & Myrtille Husband are to be free upon reaching the age of 18. |
| 1811 | Hall | Nathan | Negroes Tom-32, Esther-36, Judah-30, & Dinah-28 are hereby free on this New Year's Day 1811. |
| 1811 | Grafton | Nathaniel | In consideration of $4.00 paid by Ben Shaw, Negro, Doll, wife of Ben Shaw, is to be and henceforth is free. |
| 1811 | Enlows | James | Negro Dinah, age 28, is henceforth free. |
| 1811 | Price | Rachel | Negro Hanna-28 is hereby free on condition that she keep her children Reuben, George and Rachel until 7 yrs old. For this she is to be paid $5 per year for each child. |
| 1812 | Chew | Thomas S. | Negro Nancy, age 35, is free as of this date. |

15

# SLAVE MANUMISSIONS

| Date | Last Name | First Name | Transaction |
|------|-----------|------------|-------------|
| 1812 | Griffith | Frances | Freedom is to be granted to my Negroe, viz: Billl-43 on 1/1/13; Joe-33 on 6/1/13 ; Butler-25 on 1/1/16  Watt-23 on 1/ 1/18; Charles-14 on 1\1/18 26; Henry-1 on 1/1/1839. |
| 1812 | Willmott | Ruth | Negro Amelia is to be free at end of service to Rev. John Coleman, when 25 yrs. old: Any issue will be freed when males are 21, females 18. |
| 1812 | Weston | Rebecca | Free Negro Mingo on Aug 1 after 10 yrs. of faithful service. |
| 1812 | Loney | Mary | Negro London, age 41, is henceforth free. |
| 1812 | Hill | Aaron | Negro Fanny, age-31, is to be free on this date; Her children to be free at 22 yrs. Of age: Darkey-6, Mary-3 and Deliah-1. |
| 1812 | Gallion | Rachel | Negro Samuel, age 30, is to be free upon our demise or when he becomes 44 yrs. old. |
| 1812 | Bull | Watters | Negro Racher, age 42, is henceforth free. |
| 1812 | Bryarly | Robert | Negro Stephen-42 is hereby free; Negro Washington is to be free at end of lease to Henry Fullard on Dec. 1, 1816. |
| 1812 | Bankhead | William | Negroes are to be freed as follows: Jinny, age 28, six mos. after my decease; Yellow girl Mary and Rebecca when 18; John, Peter & Lee when 21; Robert in six mos. from this date. |
| 1812 | Ayers | Thomas | "Free Molato Jack leased to Wm. Gwyn at Monkton Mills, at the end of his service April 18, 1820. |
| 1812 | Archer | Thos., Rob't, David | Negro Matilda is hereby freed when she reaches age of 25; Any issue she has is to be free at age of 23 years. |
| 1812 | Ady | Jonathan | Negro Jack, age 43, is henceforth free. |
| 1812 | Gover | Samuel | Negro women Hagar-34 and Affy-36 are henceforth free. |

# SLAVE MANUMISSIONS

| Date | Last Name | First Name | Transaction |
|------|-----------|------------|-------------|
| 1813 | Hopkins | Rachael | Heir of George Mason; will provisions; Slaves Tuck and Nellie are to be free on the death of owner;children- boys to be free at 21, girls at 18; Stephen, William, Margard, Cassandra, Harriot, Janet, Sarah, Jacob, Lucretia, Frances,Roger, Chosey and Elizabeth. |
| 1813 | Ellis | John | Negro Priss age 44 is henceforth free. |
| 1813 | Thomas | William | Negro man Charles, commonly called Charles Johnson, is to be free forthwith. |
| 1813 | Salsbury | Daniel | Negro Peggy -40 and her girl-3 being with John Roberts are hereby free. |
| 1813 | Willmott | Sarah | Negro Abraham 26 is henceforth free. |
| 1813 | Fyllard | Henry | "In consdieration of $106", set free on this date man of color, Washington age 37. |
| 1813 | Dyer | Samuel | Negro woman Dinah 34 is henceforth free. |
| 1813 | Criswell | Mary | Negro woman Jane-25 is henceforth free and her infant son George-18 mos. is to e free at age 28. |
| 1813 | Cox | Israel | Negro boy George-13, is hereby free on Jan.1, 1825. |
| 1813 | Phillips | Martha | Negro man Jacob age 39 is henceforth free. |
| 1813 | Murango- free black | John | My daughter Catherine age 22 and her son Aquilla, given to me by Robert Jones, are henceforth free. |
| 1814 | Slade | Josias | Negro girl Hannah-12 is hereby free on her 28th birthday. |
| 1814 | Willmott | Ruth | Grant freedom to Eliza, age 9, and any offspring she may have when she is 16 yrs old. |
| 1814 | Stump | Henry | Fol. Negroes are henceforth free: Magaret-60, Joseph-58, Jack-54, June- 40, Cupid-35 and Jacob- 35. |

# SLAVE MANUMISSIONS

| Date | Last Name | First Name | Transaction |
|------|-----------|------------|-------------|
| 1814 | Rumsey | John | Fol. Negro women and my children they are hereby free: Esther-39, Grace-35, Judy-35, Hannah-31. |
| 1814 | Rodgers | Elizabeth | On paym't of 270, Negro Isaac, age 38, is hereby free. |
| 1814 | McCauley- Free black | John | Easter, the wife of John McCauley, is hereby free; Also Easter, the younger, age 20 and Mary-14. |
| 1814 | McCauley- Free black | James | "Hereby free my Negro man Charles, being my grandson whom I purchased from Mary Hall. |
| 1814 | Lytle | George | Negro Simon Bondley, age 38, is henceforth free. |
| 1814 | Kennard | Isaac | Negro Honor to be freed in 6 yrs., any male issue to be freed at age 30, females at age 25. |
| 1814 | Outton | John | Negroes Margaret-29, John-3 and Daniel-1 are hereby free. |
| 1814 | Taylor | Bennett | Negro Deliah- 20 is to be free at age 37. |
| 1814 | Kennard | Isaac | Negro girl Charlott is to be free in 21 years on June 1, 1835; Any male issue to be at 35, female at age 30. |
| 1814 | Beaven of York | Baker | Set free Negro Sarah-7 at the age of 28. |
| 1814 | Fisher | James | Negro John, age 26, is henceforth free. |
| 1814 | Garrison | Philip | Negro John-10 to be free at 28; Lucinda-7 to be free at 26. |
| 1814 | Giles | Cordelia | Negroes Clitus Moore-35 and Cliney are henceforth free. |
| 1814 | Gover of Philip | Sam | Negro man Charles, age 31, is henceforth free. |
| 1814 | Hall | William | Mulatto Henry, age 21, is hereby free. |

# SLAVE MANUMISSIONS

| Date | Last Name | First Name | Transaction |
|------|-----------|------------|-------------|
| 1814 | Hays | Cynthia | Negro woman Priscilla Elizabeth, now in possession of Charles Ward is to be set free at age 30. |
| 1814 | Archer | John, Rob.,Ste,T hom. | Negro Nat or Mat, age 44 is hereby set free. |
| 1815 | Fisher | James | Negro Jacob Hopkins, apprenticed to Robert Herr, is to gain full freedom on his 21st birthday, Oct. 1. 1817. Negro Susan-33 & her infant son, Garrett, are henceforth free; Her dau. Sarah, apprendiced to Molly Daves, is to gain full freedom on April 1, 1831. |
| 1815 | Williams- Free black | Charles | My yellow woman, Mary, being my wife, her children: David-5, James-4, Mary-5 mos. purch. Fr. Thomas Pearce of Balto. are henceforth free. |
| 1815 | Stump | Reubin | Negro Phebe-23 and her children: Jane-2 & Ruth-1 are hereby free. |
| 1815 | Rodgers Sr. | Rowland | Negro woman Molly, age 40, is henceforth free. |
| 1815 | Hall | Edward | Negro Leander, age 31, is henceforth free. |
| 1815 | Durbin- Free black | John | "For natural love and affection for my children, all males are to be free at 21, females at 16: Stephen, Grace, Mary, Hannah, Harret, Susan, Isabella, Bonaparte, Elizabeth, Christian, and Bennett. |
| 1815 | Carr | William | Negro Bib, born 2/9/1797, is to be free at age 21 [2/9/1818]. |
| 1815 | Archer Ex. Of | John | Matilda, daughter of Negro Nat & Nancy is hereby free. |
| 1815 | Quarles | John | Mytilla Husband, previously to be freed at age 18, is hereby to be freed at the age of 16. |
| 1815 | Forwood | Mary | Negro Ned, born 5/ 15/1799, is to be free at age 21. |
| 1816 | Carroll | Benjamin | Negro Jacob Spencer-28 is to be free 10 yrs from this date. |

# SLAVE MANUMISSIONS

| Date | Last Name | First Name | Transaction |
|------|-----------|------------|-------------|
| 1816 | Worthington | William | Negro Sarah-18 is hereby free; her infant Mary to be free on Nov. 1, 1831. |
| 1816 | Crigg | Edward | Negro Tisshay-25 & child Mary Jane are henceforth free. |
| 1816 | Chew | Thomas S. | Negro Priscilla, age 30 is free as of this date. |
| 1816 | Bond W. | John | Negro boy Henry, age 7 mos., is to be free at age 25. |
| 1816 | Billingslea | William | Negro Jack is henceforth free. |
| 1816 | Cox | Israel | Negro Jolly, age 21, is hereby free. |
| 1817 | Dougherty | John | Negroes are to be freed as fol: Fanny on Nov. 30, 1830; Darkey on Nov. 30, 1824; Pamaway on Nov. 30, 1831. |
| 1817 | Ady | Chloe | Wiliam Kell, age 36, is hereby free. |
| 1817 | Beatty | Frances | Negro Isaac, age 8, is sold to John McComas on condition that he is to be freed at his 31st birthday. |
| 1817 | Deaver | Mabel | Negro Jean-43 and child Maria Jane-3 are hereby free. |
| 1817 | Johns | Sarah | Negro Charles-32 is hereby free; Hannah-12 to be free 1823. |
| 1817 | Norris | Aquila | Negro Charles is to be freed on 4/1/1820 at age of 38. |
| 1817 | Sarah | Patterson | Negro Sam, under 45, is free as of this date. |
| 1817 | Courtland | George W. | Negro Tom, age 10, is to be free at age 21. |
| 1818 | Wilmott | Ruth | Negro James Parker, infant son of Lucy, is to be free on March 24, 1839. |
| 1818 | Wilson | William | Mulatto Washington-34 & Negro Milcah-33 are hereby free. |
| 1818 | Smithson | William | Negro woman Jane, age 40, is henceforth free. |

# SLAVE MANUMISSIONS

| Date | Last Name | First Name | Transaction |
|------|-----------|------------|-------------|
| 1818 | Presbury of Wm. | George | Yellow man Soloman is henceforth free. |
| 1818 | Payne | Benjamin | Rec'd $225 fr. James Wallac of York Co.. For which Negroes Betsy-20 and son Tobias-2 are free after serving Wallace until each is 28 years old. |
| 1818 | Hoopman | Christian | Negro Judy Preston, under 45, is henceforth free. |
| 1818 | Criswell | James | Negro Winston-14 is to be freed after 10 years of service. |
| 1818 | Bivens | Polly | Negro Emy is freed after serving me and my Ex. for six years from this date. |
| 1818 | Bartol | Charles | Negro Jack-17 to be freed after faithful service May '29. |
| 1818 | Allen | William | Negro Julett-16 is to be freed in 11 years; Any issue, male to be freed at 25, female at age of 21. |
| 1818 | Archer | Thomas | Fol. Negro slaves are manumitted, to wit:Jim-May, 1818; Moses,& Peg-Aug.1818; Wm.-10, George-5 & John-3- when they are age 28; Mint-8 & Rachael-6- when they are age 25; Charles-18 at age 28; Rachael-18 at age 26; Any issue, male to be freed at age 28 and female at age 25. |
| 1818 | Hendon | Sophia | Negro Rachel, age 37, is henceforth free. |
| 1818 | Wilson of John | William | Negro slaves are to be freed on Christmas Day as fol: Nance-1826, Matilda-1839; Tris-1848, Lewi-1850; Alfred-1853 Bristar-1824; Levinah-1825; Joshua-1830; Elisha-1845; Any issue male at age 30, female at 25. |
| 1819 | Dutton | John | Negro Mary, under 45, is to be free on Jan. 13, 1839 and any issue of Mary is to be free at age 28. |
| 1819 | Wilson, Heirs | Wm. | Negro woman Lydia, age 38-40, is hereby free. |

# SLAVE MANUMISSIONS

| Date | Last Name | First Name | Transaction |
|------|-----------|------------|-------------|
| 1819 | Rigdon | Stephen | Negro Nathan-21 is to be free at age of 44 in 1839. |
| 1819 | Pennington | Isaac | Negroes Chloe-31 & her ch. Millissa-5, Memmory-3, and Henry 26 days are hereby free. |
| 1819 | Hall | Edward | "Negro Phil willed to me by Thomas Hall in 1807 on cond he be freed at age 20 is hereby freed." |
| 1819 | Ford & Wollen | Wm. | Negro Robert Lingham, age 29, is to be free on 1/1/1821. |
| 1819 | Davis, Sr. | Joseph | Negro Dinah, age 36, is henceforth free. |
| 1819 | Coale | Samuel | Grant freedom to Children: of Prina: Milly & ch. Washington and Hannah; to Hannah & ch. Henry, Jane and Susan; to Susan, Betsy and Fanny, as requested by Marg't Coale. Also, as requested by my mother, M. Coale, the following slaves are hereby set free: Moses, Sarah, and Henry. |
| 1819 | Garrison | John | Black woman Rachael, age 38, is hereby free. |
| 1820 | Greenfield | Mary | Negro Harriet Murry, age 17, is to be freed at 25 or 1828. |
| 1820 | Pocock | Elijah | Negro Hager, under 45, to be free in 1825; her dau Ann is to be freed in 1845. |
| 1820 | Smith | Paca | Negro boy Isaac-9 is to be free at age of 29. |
| 1820 | Phillips | Martha | Negro woman Hannah-27 and her ch. Elizabeth & Margaret are free as of this date. |
| 1820 | Kennard | Isaac | Negro woman Jinney, age 30, is hereby free. |
| 1820 | Garrettson | Susannah | Negro woman Hannah Stevens, age 38, is hereby free. |
| 1820 | Brown | Freeborn | Negro Rachel Wilson, age 42, is hereby free. |
| 1820 | Bond | Zacheus | Negro Betty, age 30, is henceforth free. |

# SLAVE MANUMISSIONS

| Date | Last Name | First Name | Transaction |
|------|-----------|------------|-------------|
| 1820 | Ady | Chloe | Negro Phillip-20, sold to John Gellott for 23 years, is thereafter to be manumitted and set free. |
| 1820 | Ashmore | John | In consid. of $80 paid, Negro girl Lievisa-14 is free. |
| 1820 | Wilson | Thomas | Negro Sam Giles, age 22, is hereby free. |
| 1820 | Grafton | Nathniel | Fol. Are to be freed at age of 35: Ann-19, Lewis-6, Jarret-6, Mary-7, and George 3. |
| 1821 | Ashmore | John | "My colored man Aquila Montgomery", under 45, is hereby free. |
| 1821 | Taylor | Isiah | Negroes John-20 to be free at 31; Harriet-15 to be free at age of 28; Gidian-11, Andrew-10, Isaac-9 to be free at age of 30. Any issue of Harriet- male free at 30, girls are to be freed at age of 28. |
| 1821 | Rumsey | John | Negroes Prina-32 and Stephen-25 are henceforth free. |
| 1821 | Hopkins | Joseph | Negro woman Mary, age 21, is henceforth free. |
| 1821 | Dallam | Henretta | Negroes Frisby-10, Robert-8, and Tilghman-6 are to become free at the age of 30. |
| 1821 | Allender | Nicholas | Negro John Brown, age 34, is hencefoth free. |
| 1821 | Doherty | Samuel | Negro girl Fanny-14 is henceforth free. |
| 1822 | Prigg | Edward | Negroes Daniel-43, Hugh and Mulatto Markis-39 and Henney-age 35 are free. |
| 1822 | Wilson | Pamela | Negro Charlotte-34, her infant Sarah are hereby free. |
| 1822 | Wilson, et.al. | William | In con.of $100 Negro Andrew Bond is hereby set free. |
| 1822 | Waskey | Elijah | Negro Ellen Brown is apprenticed to me until 16 yrs old in 1828 by order of JP Wm. Allen and Thomas Bond. |

# SLAVE MANUMISSIONS

| Date | Last Name | First Name | Transaction |
|------|-----------|------------|-------------|
| 1822 | Gover | Robert | Negro Hannah, age 40, is hereby free. |
| 1822 | Coale | Elizabth | Negroes Jude-16 and Mark-13 are to be free at age 38; Chas Gilbert, Wm. Gilber, Eliz. Gilbert, Isaac Webster, Susannah Coale and John Herbert are freed at 38; Sarah-41 is hereby free; Hannah-10, Sarah-6, James-5, henry-2, Milly-21, George-5, Eliza-2 are to be free at 31. |
| 1822 | Ashmore | John | Fol. Negroes are hencefoth free: Samuel, Abraham and Nelly - all under 45, and Nelly's son William -3. |
| 1822 | Kennard | Isaac | Fol. Female slaves are to be free at age of 30: Harriet-20, Levina-6, Isabella-1, Malis-2 mo. Any issue, if male to be freed at 35, female at 30; harry-10, Joshua-13, Nat-3 are to be freed at age of 30. |
| 1823 | Dallam | Henretta | Fol. Negroes are to be free at age of 30: Fanny-1846; Amos-1843; Horace-1848; Henry-1853. |
| 1823 | Farmer | Richard | Negro Jeremiah, age 36, is hereby free. |
| 1823 | Maulsby | Israel | Mary Ann, 2 yr old infant of Negro Martha is to be free at the age of 30. |
| 1823 | Wilson | Pamela | Negro Jacob, 10 mos. old, is to be free at age of 21. |
| 1823 | Ashmore | John | Negro William, 2 yr old infant of Nelly's is hereby free. |
| 1824 | Gatchell | Increase | Negro Nace-19 and Mulatto Terry-9 are to be set free at age of 40; Rose-26 is to be free at 35. |
| 1824 | Whitaker | Sam'l | Negro Ledia, under 45, is hereby free. |
| 1824 | Taylor | Isaih | Negro Sarah, under 45, is hereby free. |

# SLAVE MANUMISSIONS

| Date | Last Name | First Name | Transaction |
|------|-----------|------------|-------------|
| 1824 | Robinson | William | Negro Phillis is hereby free and her ch: Alesanna-11, Louisa-8, Pamela-6, Sphia-4 to be free when each is 35; Liody-3, and James 9 mos. Are to be free when each is 21. |
| 1824 | Hall, et.al. | Anna | Negro Sarah, under 45, is hereby set free. |
| 1824 | Norris | Rhesa | Mulatto Eloiza is hereby free. |
| 1824 | Hanna | Deliverance | Negro Ned-36 is to be freed on 3/1/1832 or on my demise. Negro Henry-9 is to be free on Mar 1, 1845. |
| 1824 | Carroll | James | Negro Valentine Spencer, age 33, is hereby set free. |
| 1824 | Bond | Mary | Mulatto woman Easther, under 45, is hereby free. |
| 1824 | Norris of Jno. | John | Mulatto Mary, called Poll, is hereby set free. |
| 1825 | Prigg | Edward | $60 paid, Mulatto woman Juliott, age 17, is hereby free. $25 paid, Mulatto girl Liser, age 15, is hereby free. |
| 1825 | Bagley | Susan | Mulatto man Ned-23 is hereby free. |
| 1825 | Stevenson | Joseph | Fol. Negroes, under 45, are hereby set free: Franci Ann Brown, Suzi Brown, Cathalene Brown, William Howard. |
| 1825 | Stevenson | Joseph | Negroes Bill Harris, Henry Harris & Matilda, each being under 45, are hereby manumitted and set free. |
| 1825 | Prigg | William | Negro Charles-31 is to be free on 3/25/1831. |
| 1825 | Norris | William | Negroes Lucy and Lloyd to be free at age of 31 in '51 and '53. |
| 1825 | Johnson | Elizabeth | Negro Sharp, under 45, is hereby free. |
| 1825 | Giles | Jacob | Negro Samuel-43 is to be free on 1/1/1827. |

# SLAVE MANUMISSIONS

| Date | Last Name | First Name | Transaction |
|------|-----------|------------|-------------|
| 1825 | Clendinin | John | Negro Frances-32 is hereby free; Joshua-14 to be free in 1846, Joseph-12 in '49, when each is 35. |
| 1825 | Poteet | James | Negro Matrtha, under 45, is to be free on 6/7/1832. |
| 1826 | Dallam | William M. | Free the fol. Negro:Frank in 8 yrs., John in 10 yrs.; and Horace in 12 yrs. |
| 1826 | Worthington | Joseph | Negro Bill Bankin, age 43, is hereby free. |
| 1826 | Watters | Godfry | Negro woman Prince, age 32, is henceforth free. |
| 1826 | Smith | Paca | Negro Ellen-11 to be free at age of 29; Any offspring if male to be free at 21, female at age of 16. |
| 1826 | Matthews | Naomi | Negro Malissa, age 35, is set free as of this date. |
| 1826 | Greenfield | Henry | Fol. Negroes are to be free: Sarah-26 in 1834; John-4 in 1850; Anna-2 in 1848; Any issue male - free at 28, female issue to be free at age 25. |
| 1826 | Coale | Skipwith | Negroes Eliz. Mays, 19, John Mays-18, Ben Drummer-3 and Lucinda Mays-4 mos. are to be free at age 25. |
| 1826 | Amos | Daniel | Negro Samuel, bound to Corbin Poteet for 7 yrs. is to be free at the end of that term at the age of 26. |
| 1826 | Kenney | John W. | Negro Fanny Wells, age 40, is henceforth free. |
| 1827 | Barclay | Elizabeth | Negro Jack Burley, age 29, is to be free upon my death. |
| 1827 | Worthington | Samuel | Negro Washington-16 is to be free at 21 in 1832. |
| 1827 | Extan | Julia M. | Negro Dinah, age 40, is hereby free; Ben, age 15, is to be free at end of 10 years. |

# SLAVE MANUMISSIONS

| Date | Last Name | First Name | Transaction |
|------|-----------|------------|-------------|
| 1827 | Wilson | Joshua | Negro Hannah- 35 & child Amanda-2 are free on June first. |
| 1828 | Brown | Mary | Mulatto Hannah Bradford is hereby free. |
| 1828 | Brown | William | As of this date, Negro Rachel, called "Big Rachel" is free. |
| 1828 | Bussey | Edward | $200 paid, by Alex. Galbreath of York Co., Negro David is to be freed on 2/20/1834, being at that time under 45. |
| 1828 | Edgar-York Co. | Eleanor | Negro Peter, hired to Jas. Williams until 45, is to be freed provided he pays me $80. |
| 1828 | Ford | William | $75 paid by Harculos Wheeler & Benj. Williams, colored, Joshua Gilbert, age 21, is hereby manumitted and free. |
| 1828 | Hall | Sophia | Negro Jacob Hughes, age 40, is hereby free. |
| 1828 | Hope | Thomas | Negro Soloman, age 16, is to be free in 15 years. |
| 1828 | Rodgers | Elizabeth | Negro Nancy, under 45, formerly owned by Grandmother Priscilla Christie, is hereby free. |
| 1828 | Walker | Elizabeth | Negro Eliza, age 20, is to be free in 15 yrs. And her child Charles is to be free after 35 years of service. |
| 1828 | Smithson | William | Negro girl Jane Green, age 3, is hereby free. |
| 1828 | Wheeler- Colored | Hercules | "My daughter, Cornelia Wheeler, purchased today from Joseph Crawford, is henceforth free. She is 16 yrs. old. |
| 1829 | Hill | Aaron | Negro Charlott-29, dau. of Rebecca Frisby, is hereby free. |
| 1829 | Norris | John C. | Negro women Easter, age 38, is free as of this date. |
| 1829 | Bond | Jane | Mulatto man Stephen, under 45, is henceforth free. |

27

# SLAVE MANUMISSIONS

| Date | Last Name | First Name | Transaction |
|------|-----------|-----------|-------------|
| 1829 | Wilson | Pamela | Negro man Santy, age 30, is to be free on Jan. 1, 1830. |
| 1829 | Gorsuch | Charles | Negro Sarah-35 is hereby free; her child Mary, age 3, is to be free at age 16. |
| 1830 | Rumsey | Henretta | Negro woman Rebecca, age 38, is hereby free. |
| 1830 | Smith | Paca | Negro Rachel, age 37, is hereby free. Her children: Lydia-7, Mary-5, Charles-3, Cassa-1 are to be under the control of Joshua Husband, John Jewett, James Coale, Samuel Hopkins, Aquil Massey, David Malsby, Wm. Worthington & John Quarles ( Trustees of Deer Creek Friends Meeting) until the girls are 18 and boys are 21. when each will be free. |
| 1830 | Pitts -Colored | Peter | My wife, Susan Pitt age 32, pur. by Col Jacob Michael, is hereby free. |
| 1830 | Pitts -Colored | Isaac | Nancy Pitts, my wife, age 35, is henceforth free. |
| 1830 | Love | Margaret | Negro Peter, under 45, is hereby free. |
| 1830 | Hall | Martha | Negro man Jacob Lee, age 42, is hereby free. |
| 1830 | Kitey | Joseph | Negro man Jarrett Giles, age 20, is hereby free. |
| 1830 | Gover | Sarah | $170 paid, Negro Harriet-21 and her infant son John Richard are hereby free. |
| 1830 | Ford | William | $5 paid by Paca Gilbert, Mary Gilbert-19 is liberated 1/ 1/1831. Matildy Gilbert-17, and Charles Gilbert are hereby free. |
| 1830 | Everist | Minerva Ann | Negro Maranda-1 1is to be set free at age of 31. |
| 1830 | Cullum | Richard | Negro Sophia & her children: Maria-5 and Samuel-1 are free. |

# SLAVE MANUMISSIONS

| Date | Last Name | First Name | Transaction |
|------|-----------|------------|-------------|
| 1830 | Coale | Elizabeth | Fol. Negroes to be freed at age 30: -Moses-8, Rachael-5, Lawson-3,George-5, Eliza- 3; Any issue freed at $30; $30 paid by Negro Milly, age 29 |
| 1830 | Brown | William | Negro Barbara is hereby free; To be free at 30: Marie-20, Caroline-11, Mahale-20, Delia- 3 to be free at 21; Any issue of these to be free at 25 if girls, 35 if boys; To be free at 35:Cyrus-16, Henry-9, Sandy-5, Tom-2. |
| 1830 | Brown | Mary | Children of Rachel to be freed as fol.: Lally in 8 yrs., Polly in 2 yrs.; Rachel-14 at age 25; Moses-4 son of Lally to be free at age 21. |
| 1830 | Hall | Aquila | My Negro Isaac, hereafter Isaac Smith, age 44 is free. |
| 1831 | Griffin | John | Negro Russell Hill, age 36, is hereby free. |
| 1831 | Smith "Heirs" | Paca | " Whereas Negro Lawney did purchase Negro Abigail from Paca Smith, Abigail, age 35, & her children: John Henry-7, Michael-6, and Jacob-2, therefore they are manumitted and set free. |
| 1831 | Smith | Elizabeth | Negro Joseph Lisby, age 39, is henceforth free. |
| 1831 | Peters | Samuel | Negro Philimon Peters, age 35, is hereby set free. |
| 1831 | Bagley | Elizabeth | Negro Venus, age 35 and her children: Jane-13, Jenn-11, Grace-8, Lewis- 2, Henry-6mos. Are henceforth free. |
| 1831 | Hollis | Richard | Negro Mint, age 38, is hereby free. |
| 1831 | Cox | Samuel | Negro man James Phillips, under 45, is henceforth free. |
| 1831 | Bond | Joshua | Negro Jack Brittan, age 38, is to serve m. Maynadier for five years and then be manumitted and free. |

# SLAVE MANUMISSIONS

| Date | Last Name | First Name | Transaction |
|------|-----------|------------|-------------|
| 1831 | Miller | William | $167.50 paid, Negro Judith Thomas, age 35, is sol to Cris. Wilson for 5 yrs., Mary Thomas-14 to serve 10 yrs., & Samson Daugherty-7 to serve 21 yrs. Thereafter each is to be manumitted and set free. |
| 1832 | Prigg | Joseph | Negro slave Robert Paca-21 and Hazard Harris-43 are free. |
| 1832 | Boyd | Elizabeth | Negro Mathew is to be freed upon my decease provided faithful service is given in return. |
| 1832 | Wheeler | Hercules | Negro Amarilla Wheeler, age 22 is hereby free. |
| 1832 | Sewell | Charles  S. | Negro Rachel, age 33, is henceforth free. |
| 1832 | Rigdon | Stephen | $5 paid, Negro Ellenor, age 32, and her children: Sarah Ann-7, Mary Elenor-5, & Thos. Isreal-4 are hereby free. |
| 1832 | Renshaw | Elizabeth | $120 in hand, Negro Eliza Sutton, age 26, is to be free on 4/25/1844; Julyanna Sutton- 2mos. Is to be free 4/20/1860; Any offspring to serve 28 years. |
| 1832 | Michael | Ann | $200 in hand, Negro Peter, age 28 is hereby free. $100 paid, Abraham, 26, is henceforth free. |
| 1832 | Hoopman | Peter | Negro George Baker,age 33, is hereby free. |
| 1832 | Hays | Hannah | Negro Charlotte, age 41, is hereby free. |
| 1832 | Hall | George Wm. | Negro Jenny Hops, age 38, is hereby free. |
| 1832 | Cullum | Richard | Fol. Negroes: Mary-7, Delia-4, Sam. 18mos., are hereby free. Negro girl Hannah, age 5, is to be fee at age of 18. |
| 1832 | Cronin | William | Five dollars paid, Negro Dalia, 27, is henceforth free. |

30

# SLAVE MANUMISSIONS

| Date | Last Name | First Name | Transaction |
|------|-----------|------------|-------------|
| 1832 | Cariens | William | $25 paid, Negro Charlotte-3 is to serve Wm. Watt until12/1/1854 and then be free; $80 paid, Negro Jessee-8 is to serve Chas. Baker Hitchcock until 9/1/1855 and then be free; $50 paid, Negro woman Rainor-30 is to serve Moses St. Clair until 11/1/1838 and then be free; $50 paid, child John Rainor-1 is to serve Moses St. Clair until 5/1/1863, and thereafter be free. |
| 1832 | Barnes et al | Henry | Negro Judy Flardy, age 28, & her infant Harriet are hereby manumitted and set free. |
| 1832 | Preston -Colored | Henry | Negro Caroline, age 26, who is my property, is hereby manumitted and set free. |
| 1833 | Hutchins | Thomas | Negri Betsy, age 31, is henceforth free. |
| 1834 | Johnson | Elizabeth | Negro George, now sold to Joseph Parker for 4 yrs. Is to be free on 7/15/1838 when 26 years old; Alfred, sold to Daniel Bay for 7 years, is to be free 2/6/1841, when 27 yrs. old; David, sold to John Williams for 10 yrs.. Is to be free on 1/15/1844 when 25 yrs. old; Matilda, sold to David Pyle for 3 yrs., is to be free at end of this term when 29 yrs. old; Caroline, sold to Wm.Heaps for 8 yrs., is to be free at end of her term when 22; Nance-11 and Wm.- are to be free at 21. |
| 1834 | Gilbert | Micah | Negro Richard Herman has purchased his time and is now free. |
| 1834 | Dealer | George | Negro Avarilla, age 34, is henceforth free. |
| 1834 | Mcfadden | William | Negro Harman, age32, is henceforth free. |
| 1834 | Poteet | John | Fol. Slaves are to be freed upon my decease: Ruth-33, Arch-15, Abe-12, Sarah Ann-6 and Mary Eliz-2. |
| 1836 | Archer | Robert H. | Negro Henry Smith, age 34, is hereby free; Jim, alias James Chambers, age 30. is to be free on Jan. 1, 1837. |

31

# SLAVE MANUMISSIONS

| Date | Last Name | First Name | Transaction |
|------|-----------|------------|-------------|
| 1836 | Hitchcock | Charles | $20 on hand, Negro Louise, age 26, is free on this date. |
| 1837 | Jarrett | Jessee | Delia Alice Thompson, age 36 is hereby free. |
| 1837 | Brooke | Wiilliam R. | Negro Eliza, age about 42, is hereby free. |
| 1837 | Davis | John | Negro Harry, 32, is henceforth free. |
| 1838 | Green | Joshua | Negro Sally Preston, age 35, is hereby free. |
| 1839 | Boyd | Elizabeth | Negro Mathew Rigby, age 28, is henceforth free. |
| 1839 | Walker | Elizabeth | Negro Charlotte, age 16, is to be free at age of 36, 1859. |
| 1840 | Ford | Elizabeth | $95 in hand, Negro Sarah, age 24, is hereby free. |
| 1840 | Norris | Elizabeth | Mulatto Ann, age 32, is henceforth free. |
| 1840 | Paca-Queen Anne Co | John P. | Negro Alexander-6, son of free man Wm.Tasco of Havre de Grace & Betsy, servant of Wm. B. Paca, is now free. |
| 1841 | Allen | William | Negro Charles Flint-36 and Becky-39 are hereby free. |
| 1844 | Hall | George Wm. | Negro Frank Stokes, age 38, is hereby free. |
| 1845 | Stump | Cassandra | Negro John Dorsey, sold to Sarah Stump in 1844 for six years is hereby freed at the end of this service. |
| 1845 | Ashmore | Margaret | Negro Jim-30, is to serve Hugh Whiteford until 1849 when he is to be manumitted and set free. |
| 1846 | Foxcroft | Eliza | Negro girl Sarah, age 18, is hereby free. |
| 1847 | Dorsey | James H. | Negro Santy James, age 21, is henceforth free. |
| 1848 | Brown | Aquilla | Negroes Peter Bishop-38 and John Bishop-32 are free. |

# SLAVE MANUMISSIONS

| Date | Last Name | First Name | Transaction |
|------|-----------|------------|-------------|
| 1848 | Rogers -Heirs | Rowland | Fol. Negroes are to gain freedom upon reaching the age of 25: Lucinda-10, Mary-8 , Pinkey-3. |
| 1848 | Mathews | Naomi | $250 paid by Jacob Simms, his wife Henritta and 3 children are hereby set free. |
| 1849 | Smith - Colored | Samuel | Whereas the indenture of Negro woman Harriet Smith, age 40 and children Emeline-11 & Samuel Henry-8 were given to me, they are now and henceforth free. |
| 1849 | Stansbury | Peter | Negro Garrett Preston, age 37, is hereby free. |
| 1850 | Kennedy | James | Negro Ellisha Johnson, age 33, is hereby free. |
| 1850 | Montgomey | Mary A. | Negro Ann, age 32, left to me by Wm. Montgomery's will, is hereby free. |
| 1850 | Norris | Alexander | Negro Ruth Waters, and all issue to be born to her are free. |
| 1850 | Galloway | Abraham | Negro Wesley Bond, age 30, is henceforth free. |
| 1850 | Allen | William | Negro Martha Foremen, age 28, dau. Laura-2 |
| 1850 | Bell | David | Negro Stephen Dagan, age 21, is hereby freed. |
| 1850 | Hall | George Wm | Negro Emanuel Lee. Age 31, is hereby free. |
| 1851 | Levering | Mary Ann | Negro Margaret Jane Knah, age 40, is hereby free. |
| 1851 | Silver | Elizabeth | Fol. Negroes are henceforth free:Hariet Jones,35 and her children:Catherine-3, .Eliza-2, Ann-8 mos. |
| 1851 | Kennedy | James | Fol. Slaves are to be free at age of 26: Caroline-24, Wanda-6, Joshua-4, Benj. & George-2; Any additional offspring of girls are to be freed at age 26. |
| 1851 | Enlow | Rebecca & Temperance | Negro Elisa, age 26, and her children Hannah Matilda-2 and Ann Catherine are hereby free. |

33

# SLAVE MANUMISSIONS

| Date | Last Name | First Name | Transaction |
|------|-----------|------------|-------------|
| 1851 | Amos | Frederick T. | Negro George Lives, age 36, is henceforth free. |
| 1851 | Wilson | Joshua | $5 in hand, Negro Harriet, age 32, & her child Isabelle, 11 month old, are hereby free. |
| 1852 | Howard | Edward | Negro Isaac Dorsey, age 43, is henceforth free. |
| 1852 | Hutchins | Nicholas | Negro boy John Jamison-22 is hereby free. |
| 1852 | Norris | Eliza Jane | $5 in hand from Charles Bond, colored, Negro boy Nathan, age 11 is therefore manumitted and set free. |
| 1852 | Scott | Otho | Freedom is hereby granted to John Blackston, age 30, and Betsy Jackson, age 35. |
| 1853 | Bishop -Colored | Peter & Rachel | Freedom will be granted to fol; Negro boys at 21 yrs. Of age and to girls at 18: David-11,Joseph-10, Samuel-8, Thomas-5, Rachel-6, Elza-4. These were purc. By Mary McComas. |
| 1853 | Wilson | Rachel | Negro George Gibson, age 43, is hereby free. |
| 1853 | Bell | Nell | Negro Isaac Howard, age 30, is hereby free. |
| 1854 | Barnes | Henry | Negro saac Bishop, age 43, is hereby free. |
| 1854 | Ramply | Ann | Negro James Johnson, age 29, is hereby free. |
| 1854 | Wilson | Joshua | Negro Eliza, age 31, is hereby free as of Jan. 1, 1855. |
| 1855 | McComas | Mary | Negro Charlotte Hilton, age 30, originally intented for freedom in 1860, is hereby free as of this date. |
| 1855 | Williams | Hannah C. | Negro William Dorsey, age 30, is hereby free. |
| 1855 | Amoss | Frederick T. | Negro Maria James, age 36, is hereby free. |
| 1855 | Hall | Adaline B. | Negro Laura Johnson, age 35, is hereby free. |

# SLAVE MANUMISSIONS

| Date | Last Name | First Name | Transaction |
|------|-----------|------------|-------------|
| 1855 | Amoss | Lemuel H. | Negro girl Caroline is henceforth free. |
| 1856 | Henderson | Thomas & Alice | Negro George Henry Gover-4 and Frasnces Catherine Gover-2 are sold to Jarrett Gover, Colored, until they reach legal age for manumission and freedom. |
| 1857 | Harlan | David | Negro Emory Brown, age 39, is hereby free. |
| 1857 | Billingslea | Eliza. | Freedom is to be granted these Negroes as fol.: Woman Sidney on Bond on Dec. 25, 1867; George Bond on 12/25/1889; and Ann Bond on 12/25/1891. |
| 1857 | Guyton | Edward M. | Mulatto Ann Maria Brown, age 21, is henceforth free. |
| 1857 | Samuel Johnson, Col | Thomas W. Hall | Negro girl Susan Johnson, age 20, is henceforth free. |
| 1857 | Edward Hall | Otho Scott | As of this date, Negro Phebe and her children: Jane, Edward, Catherine, Charles, Amos, Wesley, and Mary are hereby free. |
| 1858 | Standiford | Mary & Llyod | Infant Negro slave, Mary C. Presbury, age 7 mos. Is hereby manumitted and set free. |
| 1858 | Hitchcock | Charles | Fol. Negroes are hereby freed: Ann Rose, age 35, and her children: Harriot Ross-7, Sarah Eliz. Ross-5, and Mary E. Ross-2. |
| 1858 | Galloway | Absolom | $200 paid by Stevenson Archer, Negro Henny, age 28, and her infant are to serve Archer for 7 yrs. until Henny is 35, and then are to be manumitted and set free. |
| 1858 | Haines-Colored | Joseph | The fol. Slaves, my children, are hereby free: Reuben Haines, age 30, Rachel-28, Sarah-26;Also my wife, Dinah Haines is hereby manumitted and set free. |
| 1858 | Hanna | Alexander | Negroes Augustus-7, and Charles Washington-2 are to be free at age of 28; Emily Washington-1mo. is to be free at age 18. |

# SLAVE MANUMISSIONS

| Date | Last Name | First Name | Transaction |
|------|-----------|------------|-------------|
| 1859 | Amoss | Ann & Sarah | George WashingtonTurner is to gain freedom on Jan. 31, 1863, or sooner in case of decease of either of us. |
| 1859 | Webster | John A. | Negro Margaret Lego, age 44, is hereby set free. |
| 1860 | Hanne | Robert | Negro Emily Wilson-21 & her son George Edwards-4 and any issue hereafter, shall be free at the age of 25. |
| 1860 | Whistler | William H. | My slave Bill Pinkney, age 18, is to be free at the age of 35 on April 9, 1877. |
| 1860 | Wells | Mary A. | Negroes Eliza Hughes-22, Isaac Hughes-20 & Ellen Hughes-5 are to be mamumitted and set free at the age of 35. |
| 1860 | Webster | John W. | My boy Jim Gordon-8 shall become free at age 18. |
| 1860 | Rouse | Christopher | Negro Wesley Bishop is hereby free on 1/1/1869: Good behavior will earn for said Wesley a suit of clothes and $15 cash. |
| 1860 | Richardson-Colored | Henry | "I hereby set free my wife, Harriet, age 32, and my children: Ellen-10, Wesley-8, Charles-6, George-5, David-3, Sam-1. |
| 1860 | Patterson | William | Negro boy James Bradley-17 is to be freed on on 1/1/1870. |
| 1860 | Norris | Alexander | Magaret Watters-23 is to be free on 1/1/1868. |
| 1860 | Michael | Jacob | Negro Maria Holland-32 and dau. Mary Eliz. 3, are to be manumitted and set free on May 26, 1860. |
| 1860 | Kennard | Catherine | Negro Henry is to be freed upon my natural death. |
| 1860 | Hall | George W. | Negro Lewis Paca is hereby free; Annetta Paca is to be freed on August 4, 1866. |

# SLAVE MANUMISSIONS

| Date | Last Name | First Name | Transaction |
|------|-----------|------------|-------------|
| 1860 | Hall | Adaline B. | My Negroes Edward & Hammond Taylor; Fanny Green & Philip Hollis are to be free at my death; also Susan Winchester; Fol. Minors are to be freed upon my death or on becoming of lawful age: Israel, Lawrence, Laura, Pamelia, Rebecca, Nelson. |
| 1860 | Galloway | Eugenia | Negro Laura-10 shall be manumitted and set free when she becomes 30 years old on May 29, 1880. |
| 1860 | Delmas | Henretta | My Negroes Charles Augustus and Mary Ann and any issue are to be manumitted and set free at my natural death. |
| 1860 | Courtney | Henry | Negro Howel Gibson, age 24, will hereby freed on 1/1/1874. |
| 1860 | Christie | Cornelia | Negro George Lloys Brown, age 28, is hereby free. |
| 1860 | Budd | Elizabeth | All slaves who are of lawful age-21 & 18- shall be free upon my natural death. To wit: Julia, John, Wm. Eliza, Sarah, and George Lewis; Mary Kell; Sidney, and Ann Stewart; Charles, Molly, Lizzy and Isabel Lewis who are now minors. |
| 1860 | Billingslea | Eliza | My slaves, John & Romeo, are to be set free upon my natural death. |
| 1860 | Anderson | Elizabeth | Negro Sam, age 38, is to be free on 9/1/1866 or at my death;Emily, 41, is to be free 1/1/64 or at my death. |
| 1860 | Kennard | Martha | Negro Joshua Williams is to be freed upon my natural death. |
| 1863 | Street | Thomas | Peter Stewart -Manumitted by enlisting in the regiment of Colored Troops of the Union Army 08/11/1863. |
| 1863 | Budd | Elizabeth | George M.A. Lewis - Manumitted by enlisting in the regiment of Colored Troops of the Union Army 03/24/1863. |

# SLAVE MANUMISSIONS

| Date | Last Name | First Name | Transaction |
|------|-----------|------------|-------------|
| 1863 | Webster | James | William H. Taylor -Manumitted by enlisting in the regiment of Colored Troops of the Union Army 08/11/1863. |
| 1863 | Almony | Benjamin | Jacob Smith -Manumitted by enlisting in the regiment of Colored Troops of the Union Army 03/24/1863. |
| 1863 | Finney | William | George Pikney -Manumitted by enlisting in the regiment of Colored Troops of the Union Army 11/11/1863. |
| 1863 | Bradenbaugh | Jacob | James Jones -Manumitted by enlisting in the regiment of Colored Troops of the Union Army 3/24/1863 |
| 1863 | Almony | Benjamin | William Johnson -Manumitted by enlisting in the regiment of Colored Troops of the Union Army 3/24/1863. |
| 1863 | Amos | Corbin | James Jenkins -Manumitted by enlisting in the regiment of Colored Troops of the Union Army 3/24/1863. |
| 1863 | Treadway | Julia | Stephen Jameson -Manumitted by enlisting in the regiment of Colored Troops of the Union Army. |
| 1863 | Silver | Silias | James Polk (ash Jones) -Manumitted by enlisting in the regiment of Colored Troops of the Union Army 08/24/1863. |
| 1864 | Rutledge | John | Felix Ward -Manumitted by enlisting in the regiment of Colored Troops of the Union Army 03/04/1864. |
| 1864 | Bowman | Henry | Charles Lee -Manumitted by enlisting in the regiment of Colored Troops of the Union Army 06/08/1864. |
| 1864 | Hines | James | James Maulsby -Manumitted by enlisting in the regiment of Colored Troops of the Union Army 03/24/1864. |
| 1864 | Pocock | Salem | Abraham Myers -Manumitted by enlisting in the regiment of Colored Troops of the Union Army 03/01/1864. |

# SLAVE MANUMISSIONS

| Date | Last Name | First Name | Transaction |
|------|-----------|------------|-------------|
| 1864 | Duvall | Iraminta | Washington Owens -Manumitted by enlisting in the regiment of Colored Troops of the Union Army 03/08/1864. |
| 1864 | McComas | Gabriel | Benjamin Preston -Manumitted by enlisting in the regiment of Colored Troops of the Union Army 03/24/1864. |
| 1864 | Wilson | Rachael | Silas Prigg -Manumitted by enlisting in the regiment of Colored Troops of the Union Army 03/11/1864. |
| 1864 | Scarff | Joshua | John Laurence -Manumitted by enlisting in the regiment of Colored Troops of the Union Army 03/24/1864. |
| 1864 | Preston | Eliza Ann | Moses Rice -Manumitted by enlisting in the regiment of Colored Troops of the Union Army 03/28/1864. |
| 1864 | Murphy | Mary | Samuel Heymore -Manumitted by enlisting in the regiment of Colored Troops of the Union Army 03/23/1864. |
| 1864 | Mathews | Jacob | Esau Wheeler -Manumitted by enlisting in the regiment of Colored Troops of the Union Army 03/24/1864. |
| 1864 | Forward | Parker | Dick Williams -Manumitted by enlisting in the regiment of Colored Troops of the Union Army 04/26/1864. |
| 1864 | Smithson | Thomas | George Wye -Manumitted by enlisting in the regiment of Colored Troops of the Union Army 03/31/1864. |
| 1864 | Smithson | Thomas | John Richard Wye -Manumitted by enlisting in the regiment of Colored Troops of the Union Army 03/31/1864. |
| 1864 | Preston | Eliza Ann | Alexander Rice -Manumitted by enlisting in the regiment of Colored Troops of the Union Army 03/28/1864. |
| 1864 | Bradford | I.T. | Absomalom Davis -Manumitted by enlisting in the regiment of Colored Troops of the Union Army 1/1/1864. |

# SLAVE MANUMISSIONS

| Date | Last Name | First Name | Transaction |
|------|-----------|------------|-------------|
| 1864 | McComas | Gabriel | Jacob Brown -Manumitted by enlisting in the regiment of Colored Troops of the Union Army 03/24/1864. |
| 1864 | Street | Priscilla | Solomon Clark -Manumitted by enlisting in the regiment of Colored Troops of the Union Army 03/29/1864. |
| 1864 | Hutchins | John | Benjamin Cromwell -Manumitted by enlisting in the regiment of Colored Troops of the Union Army 03/24/1864. |
| 1864 | Rutledge | John | George W. Jackson -Manumitted by enlisting in the regiment of Colored Troops of the Union Army 03/24/1864. |
| 1864 | Hutchins | John | Richard Cromwell -Manumitted by enlisting in the regiment of Colored Troops of the Union Army 03/24/1864. |
| 1864 | Keen | Sarah | Harry C. Billingslea -Manumitted by enlisting in the regiment of Colored Troops of the Union Army 03/28/1864. |
| 1864 | Street | Abram | Abraham Evans -Manumitted by enlisting in the regiment of Colored Troops of the Union Army 03/24/1864. |
| 1864 | Silver | Henry | Leander Green -Manumitted by enlisting in the regiment of Colored Troops of the Union Army 02/02/1864. |
| 1864 | Rutledge | John | Henry Harris -Manumitted by enlisting in the regiment of Colored Troops of the Union Army 03/24/1864. |
| 1864 | Rutledge | John | Isaac Harris -Manumitted by enlisting in the regiment of Colored Troops of the Union Army 03/24/1864. |
| 1864 | Hitcock | William | Lewis Harris -Manumitted by enlisting in the regiment of Colored Troops of the Union Army 03/10/1864. |
| 1864 | Rutledge | John | Edgar Hayden -Manumitted by enlisting in the regiment of Colored Troops of the Union Army 03/24/1864. |

40

# SLAVE MANUMISSIONS

| Date | Last Name | First Name | Transaction |
|------|-----------|------------|-------------|
| 1864 | Preston | Fanny | Moses Howard -Manumitted by enlisting in the regiment of Colored Troops of the Union Army 03/24/64. |
| 1864 | Hutchins | John | Joshua Cromwell -Manumitted by enlisting in the regiment of Colored Troops of the Union Army 03/24/1864. |
| 1865 | Rutledge | Abraham | Benjamin Johnson -Manumitted by enlisting in the regiment of Colored Troops of the Union Army 08/31/1865. |
| 1865 | Amos | James | Albert Berry -Manumitted by enlisting in the regiment of Colored Troops of the Union Army 08/031/1865. |
| 1865 | Munikysen | William | Henry -Manumitted by enlisting in the regiment of Colored Troops of the Union Army 08/29/1865. |

# SLAVE SALES

# SLAVE SALES

| Date | Seller First Name | Seller Last Name | Buyer First Name | Buyer Last Name | Price | Transaction |
|---|---|---|---|---|---|---|
| 1775 | Cpt. William | Richardson | Aquilla | Hall | 32:18:10 | One Negro boy named Jim, age 11. |
| 1776 | J. Sam'l | Dooley | Francis | Davis | 50 pounds | Negro woman Phillis and sons: Abe-4 and Benn 2. |
| 1777 | John | Dorsey | James | Maxwell | 5 shillings sterling | For use of Ann Dorsey, Negro woman Belinda and her son Luke; One roan and black horse. |
| 1777 | Joseph | Renshaw | Thomas | Street | 200 pounds | Ten Negroes: Solomon, Cato, Jerr, Afey, Doll, Mall; Children: Bet, Janey, Jack and Jim. |
| 1778 | Mary Lynch | Sims | Dr. Thaddeus | Jewett | 300 pounds PA money | Negro Jenny given to Mary L Simms by her father Dr. James Lee. |
| 1778 | Josiah | Hichcock | Isaac | Montgomery | 69 pounds | One Negro girl Meriah, age 14 months. |
| 1778 | Josiah | Hichcock | James | Pocock | 100 pounds | One Negro girl Ruth, age 8 months. |
| 1778 | Mary | Lynch | John | Lynch | 5 shillings | Negroes Sal & Hagar to be del when John is 21; Negro Dinah to be delivered upon my death. |
| 1779 | Wm | McGuire | James | Cain | 100 pounds | One Negro wench Milly. |
| 1779 | Ann | Amos | Susannah | Amos | Love & aff | One Negro girl Jane. |

45

## SLAVE SALES

| Date | Seller Last Name | Seller First Name | Buyer Last Name | Buyer First Name | Price | Transaction |
|------|------------------|-------------------|-----------------|------------------|-------|-------------|
| 1779 | Clark | Robert | Morgan | William | 254:08:11 | Negro woman Pugg and her daughter Heagar. |
| 1781 | Bosley | William | Hall | Josias | | Exchange-Negro wench Hagar for Negro wench Len. |
| 1782 | Billingslea | Walter | Billingslea | Ruth | ?? | Rachael and Ben children of Negro Phoebia, also one Negro boy called Jack. |
| 1782 | Moore | John | Mather | Michael | 55 pounds | One Negro girl Violet, age 8. |
| 1784 | Smith | Henry | Wheeler | Ignatius | 15 pounds & other | Negroes: Roger, Bill, Ned, Jacob, Ralph, and Harry. One blooded mare and one Negro boy. |
| 1784 | Hichcock | Josiah | Hichcock | Randall | 310 pounds | Negroes: Hannah-26, Graw-20, Dinah & Phobe-2 and Lydia, 6 months. |
| 1784 | Seale | Priscilla | Cowan | Alexander | 60 pounds | One Negro boy named Jack. |
| 1784 | Jemkins | John | Walters | Henry | 7 pounds | Negro man Dick; girls : Abaigail, Pat and Phillis; boys: Harry and Cesar. |
| 1784 | Hawkins | Robert | Wheeler | Ignatius | 300 pounds | Negroes: Alice-19, Elleck-9, Beck-3 and Jamos. |

46

# SLAVE SALES

| Date | Seller Last Name | Seller First Name | Buyer Last Name | Buyer First Name | Price | Transaction |
|------|------------------|-------------------|-----------------|------------------|-------|-------------|
| 1784 | Hawkins | Samuel | | Pompey | 17 pounds | Sold to Negro Pompey, late servant of William Hopkins, Negro Sarah and children James and Elijah. |
| 1784 | Carlile | Lancelot | Whiteford | Robert | 25 pounds | One young Negro girl, Fanny. |
| 1785 | Dorsey | John | Maxwell | Moses | 110 pounds | Two Negroes: Joe and Belinda. |
| 1785 | Dorsey | J.Hammond | Maxwell | Moses | 80 pounds | Negro Abraham. |
| 1786 | Carile | Lancelot | Rutledge | Jacob | 30 pounds | One Negro boy Bob age 7. |
| 1786 | Carile | Lancelot | Bull | John | 37:10:00 | Negro Fanny age 46. |
| 1786 | Smithson | Archibald | Orrick-Balt Co Merchant | John | 85:18:03 | Negro girls Bet and Hannah; Negro boy Tom. One bay horse called "Bloody Buttocks". |
| 1787 | Scott | James | Harris | Robert | 93:01:03 | One Negro wench named Phebey. |
| 1787 | Carlile | Robert | Amos | James | 70 pounds | One Negro man named Tom. |
| 1787 | Cowan | Alexander | Boyce | Roger | 860 pounds | Negroes: Jack, Dick,James Aaudelin, Grace, Rose; children: Tom, Jack, Nan, Fran, Sarah, and Sophia. |

47

# SLAVE SALES

| Date | Seller Last Name | Seller First Name | Buyer Last Name | Buyer First Name | Price | Transaction |
|------|------------------|-------------------|-----------------|------------------|-------|-------------|
| 1787 | Ditto | Willliam | Ditto | Abraham | 200 pounds | Negroes: Mint, Poll, Nan, Harry, Charles, Ben, Isaac, Pegg, Natt and Hannah; Also 3 horses, 2 cows and furniture. |
| 1787 | Greenfield | Thomas | Vansickles | Henry | Estate of P Kimball | Negroes: Phill, Peter, Bill, Pegg, Cass, Poll, Bet, Patience, and Dark. |
| 1787 | Love | John | Bunting | Billy | 31 pounds | One mulatto man named Tom. |
| 1787 | Greenfield | Thomas | Vansickle | Henry | 40 pounds | One Negro named Hamed age 12. |
| 1788 | Day | Wm Fell | Fulton | John | 150 pounds | Silver watch, Negro woman Phebe; ch: Poll, Sal, Meta, Ben; 3 horses, 4 cows, 8 sheep, 3 lambs, 6; hogs, sundry items. |
| 1789 | McComas | Alexander | Lytle | Wm Bradford | 5 shillings | Negro woman Jude and girl Sarah. |
| 1789 | Osborn | Benjamin | Garrettson | Freeborn | 94:17:02 | Two Negro men Jack and George. |
| 1789 | Hudson | James | Maxwell | Jacob | 15 pounds | Negro girl Charlotte age 3. |

# SLAVE SALES

| Date | Seller Last Name | Seller First Name | Buyer Last Name | Buyer First Name | Price | Transaction |
|---|---|---|---|---|---|---|
| 1790 | Maxwell | Moses | Maxwell | Jacob | 1068:15:00 | Negroes: Charles, Joe, Abe, Jenny, Belinda, Sall: Children: Lurain, Tom, Pacolett, Nat and Charles; Also 25 cattle, 19 sheep, 13 horses, 3 feather beds, desk, bookcase, cherry table, walnut table, chest of drawers, Schooner called "Brothers" w tow boat, batteau, sails and riggin, one old clock. |
| 1790 | Smith | Elizabeth | Smith | William | 5 shillings | Negro Rachael and child; Tom, Bill, Benn, Nance, Poll, Dinah. |
| 1791 | Pocock | Daniel | Pocock | David | 65:05:00 | To Son, David Negroes Stephen and Martha; Also all my livestock and household goods. |
| 1791 | Downing | Samuel | Wheeler | Ignatius | 46:15:05 | One Negro wench called Poll. |
| 1791 | Little | George | Contee for Alexander Contee | Thomas | 375 pounds | Negroes: Darkee-35, Hagar-25, Harry-11, Jacob-6, Nat-6, Aquila-3, Milcah-8, Fanny-3 and Rachael-1; Also Negro boys: Peter-20 and James-20. |
| 1791 | Pocock | Daniel | Pocock | Elijah | Love & aff | One Negro woman Cate and girl Hagar. |
| 1791 | Pocock | Daniel | Pocock | Charlotte | love & aff | One Negro girl Phebe. |

# SLAVE SALES

| Date | Seller Last Name | Seller First Name | Buyer Last Name | Buyer First Name | Price | Transaction |
|------|------------------|-------------------|-----------------|------------------|-------|-------------|
| 1792 | Contee | Thomas | Osborn | William | 120 pounds | Negroes James & Peter ( named in George Little mortgage). |
| 1792 | Debrular | William | Day | John | 100 pounds | Negroes: Phebe & child Sophia; Livestock and personal gds. |
| 1792 | Love | John | Billingslea | Walter | 41:05:06 | One Negro man Cato. |
| 1793 | Contee | Thomas | Little | George | 112:10:00 | Negroes: Aqila, Jacob, Milcah, Fan & Rachael. |
| 1793 | Turner | Daniel | Webster& John Lee | Samuel | Rent Due & 40 pounds | Negroe girl Joan 7 boy Bob-6;40 bu corn, 12 ton hay. |
| 1793 | Turner | Daniel | Turner | Jacob | 200 pounds | Negroes William-18 & Joan-14, 2 feather beds, 1 desk, 2 tables, 6 chairs, 2 horses, 3 cows 12 sheep and 12 hogs. |
| 1793 | Turner | Daniel | Turner | Levi | 150 pounds | Negroes Sam-12, Nance-12 Also 2 feather beds, 1 desk, 2 tables, 6 windsor chairs and 4 horses. |
| 1793 | Osborn | James | Chauncy | George | 180 pounds | Negroes Hagar, Doll, Connie, Samson, Isaac, Nab and Jack. |
| 1793 | Osborn | James | Osborn | Cyrus | 150 pounds | Negroes: Black Priss, yellow Priss, Harry, Fan and Nance. |

50

# SLAVE SALES

| Date | Seller Last Name | Seller First Name | Buyer Last Name | Buyer First Name | Price | Transaction |
|---|---|---|---|---|---|---|
| 1793 | Osborn | James | Hanson | John | 182:10:00 | Negroes: Bill Moore, Bill Dongo, Prince, Gus & Frank. |
| 1793 | Little | George | Gough | Henry | 89 pounds | Negores Hagar, Nat and Stephen. |
| 1793 | Gover | Robert | McFade-of Baltimore City | John | 169:01:07 | Negroes: Roger-30, Sarah-25, Judy-12, Leander-9 Roger-7, and Tom-6. |
| 1793 | Contee | Thomas | Little | George | 89 pounds | Negroes Hagar, Nat and Stephen. |
| 1794 | Moford | Thomas | Clark | John | 100 pounds | Negro Jim, Rachael & her issue, 1 cow and calf, 1 bed. |
| 1794 | Gover | Priscilla | Prall | Edward | 200 pounds | Negroes James, Ester, Polly, Mame: ch: Poll, James, Delia;Also 5 Havre de Grace lots, share in fathers estate 2 feather beds, case of drawers & dining room table. |
| 1794 | Bateman | William | Birkhead | Matther | 50 pounds | Negroe girl Sarah-16; 1 bed & furniture, 2 horses, saddles & bridles, farming tools and household goods. |
| 1794 | McComay | Edw | Lowery & George Cunningham | James | 174:15:00 | Negro woman Ester and her child;also 2 horses, 1 cow, set blacksmith tools, household furniture and one lot in Abingdon. |

51

# SLAVE SALES

| Date | Seller Last Name | Seller First Name | Buyer Last Name | Buyer First Name | Price | Transaction |
|---|---|---|---|---|---|---|
| 1794 | Bond, sheriff | James | Strong | Joseph | 03:16:09 | Negro Limus taken and sold for tax purposes. |
| 1794 | Chamberlain | Jon | Galloway | Absolom | 50 pounds | Negro Charlotte and her child Charles. |
| 1794 | Raine | Samuel | Raine | Sarah | 30 pounds | Negro woman - Terry-30 and James-5. |
| 1794 | Gover | Phillip | Cooper | Thomas | 65 pounds | One Negro boy named William. |
| 1794 | Money | Robert | Money | Samuel | 200 pounds | Negroes Rebecca-18, Peregrine-16 and Frances-14;2 cows, w horses, 23 hogs, 50 bu corn, 2 feather beds, 3 pots, Dutch oven, kittle, griddle & grill, brass skilet, desk, one cart, plow and harrow, one stack of corn. |
| 1794 | Gover | Phillip | Huges | Everett | 45 pounds | One mulatto boy Harry, age 11. |
| 1794 | Hay | John | Hay - son | John | love & aff | Negroes Sharper, James Perry, Sal and Judah. All my livestock and household goods. |
| 1794 | Hudson | James | York | Mary | 40 pounds | One Negro slave called Abraham. |

52

# SLAVE SALES

| Date | Seller Last Name | Seller First Name | Buyer Last Name | Buyer First Name | Price | Transaction |
|---|---|---|---|---|---|---|
| 1794 | Manner | Alexander | Stansbury-Balt Cty | Edward | 100 pounds | One Negro Harry also livestock (horses, cows, sheep, hogs) 1 bed, w iron pots, Dutch oven, chest, spinning wheel & reel, 2 flat irons, & various farm tools and grain. |
| 1794 | Crockett-Balt Co | Benjamin | Hill | George | 145:10:00 | Negro Ester-50, Joh-10, Molly-12 and Ann-7. |
| 1795 | Jeffry | Robert | Prall | Edward | Debts Due | Negroes Nan, Charles 7 Hagar; Also one team of horses 7 wagon, one Marocco pocket book. |
| 1795 | Gallion | John | Vansickle | Henry | 30 pounds | Negro Scipio age 20. |
| 1795 | Gover | Gerrard | Hammond, Balt.Co | Wm | 120 pounds | Negroes Harry-33 and Dander-23. |
| 1795 | Giles | Elizabeth | Gover | Philip | 5 shillings | Negro Darby & Nancy, girls Polly, Fanny and Ruth;Also various and sundry farm and household goods. |

## SLAVE SALES

| Date | Seller Last Name | Seller First Name | Buyer Last Name | Buyer First Name | Price | Transaction |
|---|---|---|---|---|---|---|
| 1795 | Gover | Gerrard | Giles | Elizabeth | 200 pounds | Negroes Darby and Nancy, girls: Polly, Fanny & Ruth; Also 4 horses, cart, 4 cows, 20 hogs, table, desk,beds 7 bedding, 16 table cloths & towels, earthen dishes & plates, knives 7 forks, looking glass, pr andirons, shovel, tongs, 3 hoes, grindstone, 2 axes, 3 soup pots, 8 waiters, Dutch oven, 3 tubs, 4 water pails, 100 lb bacon, 35 barrels corn, 11 windsor chairs, 2 tea kettles, sundry tea ware, 2 guns. |
| 1795 | Rockhold - Delaware Co PA | John | Bond | John | 50 pounds | Negro Nancy York and her child Rachael to serve until each reaches the age of 31 then to be set free. |
| 1795 | Gover & others | Gerrard | Shoemaker | Edward | 400 pounds | Negroes Darby, Nancy, Barbary, Polly, Fanny, Ruth & Charlot;Also 5 horses, 4 cows, 2 calves, pr oxen, 20 sheep, 20 hogs, 2 beds, 8 table cloths, 4 towels, 2 plows, 3 hoes, 1 desk,8 jJapaned tea boards, bedstead, pr tongs & shovel, 3 pots, 2 Dutch ovens, table and tea ware, 4 carpets, 2 large tables, small table, one cart and 3 harnesses, sundry other goods. |
| 1795 | Bond,Sheriff | John | Stong | Joseph | 04:04:01 | Negro man London sold for taxes owned by Thomas Strong. |

## SLAVE SALES

| Date | Seller Last Name | Seller First Name | Buyer Last Name | Buyer First Name | Price | Transaction |
|------|------------------|-------------------|-----------------|------------------|-------|-------------|
| 1795 | Bond,Sheriff | John | Strong | Joseph | 06:02:06 | Negro Will-13, Sold for taxes owed by Thomas Strong. |
| 1795 | Wood | James | Hampton | Michael | 25 pounds | One Negro girl named Harriet. |
| 1796 | Wells | Jane | Jolley | John | 60 pounds | One Negro man named Jerry. |
| 1796 | Thompson | Cynthia | Dunham | John | 120 pounds | Following purchased at indicated prices: Negro Affy-30 pounds; boy Tower - 10 pounds, boy Wm - 15 pounds, child Samson -02 pounds, lad Pomphrey - 22:10:00, boy George - 03 pounds - 03 pounds; desk 05:00:00, 3 beds - 10 pounds, sorrel horse-18:15:00, cow & calf - 04:10:00. |
| 1796 | Onion | Corbin | Onion | Tthomas | 375 pounds | Negroes Jacob, Phebe 7 child; all stock on the farm. |
| 1796 | Barton | William | Low | Jessee | 25 pounds | Negro Luke-13 for 21 yrs, thereafter he is to be free. |
| 1796 | Brooke | Richard | Prigg | Edward | 150 pounds | Negro girl Nance & boy James; one gelding w saddle, set silver tea spoons, one bed and furniture. |
| 1796 | Gover | Phillip | Evit | Margaret | 60 pounds | One Negro wench Hannah. |

55

**SLAVE SALES**

| Date | Seller Last Name | Seller First Name | Buyer Last Name | Buyer First Name | Price | Transaction |
|------|------------------|-------------------|-----------------|------------------|-------|-------------|
| 1796 | Gover | Robert | Tolley | John | 45 pounds | Negro Cesar age 30. |
| 1796 | Norris | Jacob | Norris | John | 64 pounds in gold & silver | Negro woman Judy, girls Cass & Polly; also all the cows, horses, sheep & hogs, farming equipt; household 7 kitchen goods, raw hides 7 leather, corn and wheat in the ground, 1 still; all goods on Norris farm. |
| 1796 | Prall | Edward | Thompson | James | $38.00 | Negro woman Nan and girls Lily and Judy. |
| 1796 | Raphel | Stephen | McCurdy | Hugh | 196 pounds | Negroes Sam-25, Teague-22, Hass-18, Ann-32, & Sophia-17. |
| 1796 | Harris | Robert | Miller | Joseph | 116 pounds | Negroes Charlotte, George & Frank; six horses, yoke oxen 5 cattle; all my household furniture. |
| 1796 | Rumsey | John | Turner | Andrew | 55 pounds | Negro Sal to serve 9 years and any issue until age 31. |
| 1797 | Daugherty | John | Taylor | Ashberry | $100.00 | Negro boy Shadrack. |
| 1797 | Michael | James | Michael | Daniel | 38 pounds | One Negro slave named Phebia. |
| 1797 | Hopkins | Charles | Money | Samuel | 30 pounds | One male slave named Perry, age 19. |

56

## SLAVE SALES

| Date | Seller Last Name | Seller First Name | Buyer Last Name | Buyer First Name | Price | Transaction |
|------|------------------|-------------------|-----------------|------------------|-------|-------------|
| 1797 | Hichcock | Josiah | Hichcok-Balt Co | William | 245:15:08 | Negro girls: Dinah, Phebe, Hannah, and Elizabeth Negro boys: Edward, John and Joshua. |
| 1797 | Hammond- Balt Co | Wm | Gover | Gerrard | 68:15:00 | Negro man Harry, age 35. |
| 1797 | Beaty | Archibald | Smith | Winstone | 150 pounds | Negroes Tom-30, Solomon-21, William-12, Philip-11. |
| 1797 | Wheeler | Hennrette & Ignatius | Bailey- Balt Town | William | 60 pounds | One Negro girl Sal age 15. |
| 1797 | Money | Samuel | Hambleton | John | 35 pounds | One negro boy Frank age 14. |
| 1797 | Allender | John | Garrettson | Ruth | 100 pounds | Negro slave Bill to serve 10 years & then to be free. |
| 1797 | Money | Samuel | Hambleton | John | 40:07:02 | One Negro slave named Perry age 19. |
| 1798 | Gover | Robert | Young of Balt Co | William | 30 pounds | Negro boys: James -6 and Ben-4. |
| 1798 | Lee | Josiah | Lee | James | 300 pounds | Negoes: Parroway-45, sesar-47, Poll-45, Priss-30, Luke-8, Parroway-7, Duke-3 and Hanna-1. |
| 1798 | Smith | Winston | Christie | Gabriel | 62:10:00 | Negro man Daniel (willed to me by Susanna Scott). |

## SLAVE SALES

| Date | Seller Last Name | Seller First Name | Buyer Last Name | Buyer First Name | Price | Transaction |
|------|------------------|-------------------|-----------------|------------------|-------|-------------|
| 1798 | Dorsey | Matthew | Hall Lee | Parker | 200 pounds | Negro women: Sarah-18, Nan-19, girls: Jane-13, Patience age 10 boys: Harry-8. Seven horses, yoke oxen and ox cart, and other goods. |
| 1798 | Michael | Daniel | Michael | James | 38:02:6 | One Negro Phebe also 5 horses, 2 mules, 9 cattle, yoke oxen & cart, 2 feather beds & furniture. |
| 1798 | Taylor | Ashberry | Whitaker | Isaac | 37:10:00 | One Negro slave Shadrack age 15. |
| 1798 | Michael | James | Taylor | Ashberry | 70 pounds | Negro Hannah-33 and her child Leander -4 months. |
| 1798 | Anderson | William | Anderson | James | 120 pounds | One Negro woman Nell, case of drawers, 3 beds, 2 tables, 6 chairs, 18 puter plates & 1 dish, iron pot 7 baker. |
| 1799 | Marche | John | Onion | Thomas Bond | 506 pounds | Negroes: William-12, Llyod-4, Milley-6; Four horses, pair oxen & cart, 7 cattle, 8 sheep, 35 hogs, 2 ploughs, 6 silver table spoons, 12 silver tea spoons, 2 silver tongs, butter toasts, cream jug, pepper boxes, 3 beds, chest drawer, 2 mahony table, 2 saddles & bridles, 25 pound yarn, cutting box, other utensils & goods. |

58

## SLAVE SALES

| Date | Seller Last Name | Seller First Name | Buyer Last Name | Buyer First Name | Price | Transaction |
|---|---|---|---|---|---|---|
| 1799 | Wheeler | Benner | Morgan | Robert | 25 pounds | Negroes: Robin- 60, Sara-60: Also Feather bed, beds't, breakfast table, frying pan, pot rack, 3 plows, 3 pr iron chains, 4 leather collars, 2 ox chains, 8 barrels corn, 300 lb bacon, 5 hoes, 2 mallick, croe bar, flax unbroke, cider mill & casks, wheat fan, 20 bu llime, grindstone, saddles, bridles, desk. |
| 1799 | Smithson | Daniel | Howard | Dorsey | 50 pounds | One stud horse, w cows & calves, sow & 7 pigs, Negro girl named Sharlott, case drawers, 2 beds, walnut table, 5 chairs, 2 chests, spinning wheel, pair hames, 2 pots, Dutch oven, 12 pewter plates, dish and basin, 6 china plates, 6 knives & forks, 2 saddles, 2 chairs, 2 tubs, 3 piggins, hoes, 5 shovels, 10 bu potatoes, corn, oats, and flax growing in the fields. |
| 1799 | Scott | Daniel | Smithson | William | 10 pounds | Negroes: Phillis, Rose.Sam, Bert,& Jach; girls: Dinah, Hannah, Rose, boys: Samson, John, Nero, Ben. |
| 1799 | Wheeler | Joseph | Hall, Bal Co | John | 50 pounds | Negroes Harry and Tom. |
| 1799 | Webster | John Lee | Ruff | John | 137:17:0 | Negroes: Lawney, Pompey, Moses, Ben and Tark. |

59

## SLAVE SALES

| Date | Seller Last Name | Seller First Name | Buyer Last Name | Buyer First Name | Price | Transaction |
|---|---|---|---|---|---|---|
| 1800 | Osborn | James | Chauncy | George | $400 | Negroes: Bill Moore, Bill Dango, Prince, Frederick, and Gustus. |
| 1800 | Osborn | James | Chauncy | John | $250 | Yellow Priss, Black Priss, Harry, Fan and Nance. |
| 1800 | Worthington | Joseph | Mahon | Elizabeth | 30 pounds | Negro Priss (Formerly owned by Charles Worthington). |
| 1800 | Durham | Thomas | Young | Hugh | 200 pounds | Negroes: Nance, Delia, Celia, Abraham & Benjamin. |
| 1800 | Luckie | John | Wallace | Jjames | $200 c.m. | Services of Mulatto Martin, age 10, until he is 28 years of age when he is to be set free. |
| 1800 | McComas | John | Onion | Thos Bond | 60 pounds | One Negro boy Joseph. |
| 1801 | Everest | Samuel | Howard | leonard | $300 | One Negro man named Jack. |
| 1801 | Osborn | Benjamin | Osborn | William | $150 | One Negro girl Priss until free by manumission; Also various and sundry stock & household articles. |
| 1801 | Forwood | John | Ady | William | 50 pounds | One Negro Prilla, age 9. |

# SLAVE SALES

| Date | Seller Last Name | Seller First Name | Buyer Last Name | Buyer First Name | Price | Transaction |
|------|------------------|-------------------|-----------------|------------------|-------|-------------|
| 1801 | Mitchell - Balt Co | Francis | Wheeler | Bennett | 93:15:00 | One Negro girl Rachael, age 9; one boy Joe age 6; one sorrel mare, age 5. |
| 1802 | Sappington | Richard | Jones | Stephen | $100 silver | Negro woman Nan, age 25. |
| 1802 | Smith | John | Jolley | John | $100 lawful m. | Negro Samuel, age 11 ( formerly owned by Marg Dallam). |
| 1802 | Wheeler | Benj | Water | Samuel | 100 pounds | Negro man Frank and boy Paul; also sundrey goods and chattel. |
| 1803 | Biddle- Balt City | Richard | Barton | John | 13:10:00 | One Negro lad, Nace, age 15. |
| 1803 | Preston-Balt Co | Corbin | Jarrett | Bennett | 46 pounds | Negro man named Ben. |
| 1803 | Miles | Aquila | Rutledge | Josua | $35 | Negro lad Ignatius, age 16. |
| 1803 | Criswell | Robert | Parsons- free Negro | Caleb | 23 pounds | One Negro boy Moses, age 6. |
| 1803 | Amos | James | Bulter | Thomas | $200 | Negro woman Cass; stock farm and household goods. |
| 1803 | Griffith | Sarah | Howard | Leonard | $400 | Negro Sarah, age 24 7 her ch: Joe-4, Dock-3, Harriet. |

# SLAVE SALES

| Date | Seller Last Name | Seller First Name | Buyer Last Name | Buyer First Name | Price | Transaction |
|---|---|---|---|---|---|---|
| 1804 | Prichard | Ann | Stephenson | James | $179.72 | One Negro girl Hannah and one brown mare. |
| 1804 | Jarrett | Bennett | Street | John | 45 pounds | One Negro man Ben. |
| 1804 | Wheeler | Bennett | Bond | John C. | 15:19:06 | Two feather beds, bedstead, desk, chest, cherry table, Negro woman Sal & Negro man Robin. |
| 1804 | Welch | William | Moore | John | 28:06:02 | Negro Sam age 21, girl Silvey age 4, Dun mare-6, brown horse-6, and sorrel colt. |
| 1804 | Taylor | James | Taylor | Isaih | $300.00 | Negro women Sall, boy John age 4, and child Hariot. |
| 1804 | McComas | Nicholas | Macatee | Henry | 7;:10:00 | Negro boy Ben. |
| 1804 | Carroll | Benjamin | Duly-Abingdon | Wm | $34 | Negro Jacob, age 17 & one pair wool mittens. |
| 1804 | Carroll | Benjamin | Hudson | James | 45 pounds | Negro boys: Jacob, Daniel, Jonas; also sundry goods. |
| 1804 | Nelson | Aquila | Taylor | James | 200 pounds | Negro Shadrack & woman Sall; Also cart & oxen, 4 cows, 12 hogs, 3 horses, and various farm & household goods. |

**SLAVE SALES**

| Date | Seller Last Name | Seller First Name | Buyer Last Name | Buyer First Name | Price | Transaction |
|------|------------------|-------------------|------------------|-------------------|-------|-------------|
| 1805 | Ford | Joseph | Ford | Mary | 22:08:06 | Negro boy Aaron, age 12. |
| 1805 | Galloway-Balt Co | Robet | Murray | William | $1.00 | Negro woman Sal. |
| 1805 | Howlett | John | Smith | John | 250 pounds | Negro man Hampton, 2 bay horses, wagon & grears, 2 pr. Traces, 2 brown cows, 500 hides, 10 dozen skins, 30 cord tanbark, tanyard tools & currying tools, etc. |
| 1805 | Jay | Samuel | Boyer | Roger | $100.00 | One Negro Joe, age 26 and one black horse. |
| 1805 | Johnson | James | Hokins | Ephraim | 65 pounds | Negroes George, Clara, Mount & Chaelotte, conveyed by Eprhaim Gettings Gover to Joseph Worthington. |
| 1805 | Saunders | Robert | Holland & James Hunter | Edward | 200 pounds | Negroes: man Emanuel; boy Phil; girls Doll, Maria, and Lucy. Buyers from AACo. |
| 1805 | Woolsey | George | Moore | Susan | 40p, Md. Money | One Negro girl, Vioteo. |
| 1805 | Watkins | Tobias | Hall | Wm. & Edw | Debt & 5a | Mulatto boy Lewis, age 8. |
| 1806 | Stump | Henry | Hopkins | Samuel | 30 pounds | One Negro woman, Hannah. |

## SLAVE SALES

| Date | Seller Last Name | Seller First Name | Buyer Last Name | Buyer First Name | Price | Transaction |
|---|---|---|---|---|---|---|
| 1806 | Norris | Charles | Murphy | John | $250.00 | Negro girls: Hannah, Dianna, Mararet also, four feather beds. Buyer from Fells Point. |
| 1807 | Ford | Joseph | Ford - bro | Joshua | 5 shillings | Negroes Isaac and Darkey for life: Son John to serve until 21 and then manumitted; Also Abigail to serve 6 years, Teany for 7 yrs., Sophia fo 16 yrs., Solomon for 21 yrs., & Henry for 23 yrs., therafter each is to be manumitted and set free. |
| 1807 | Ford | Joseph | Deaver- sister | Mabel | 5 shillings | Negro Mary to serve 5 yrs. And then to be set free; Any issue, male to serve until 28, female until 22. |
| 1807 | Moore | Jason | Moore. | Susan | 150p. of Md. | Negroes Minty, James and Alice. |
| 1807 | Norris | James | McComas | Josiah | 127:10:00 | Negro man Mingo, age 27 & woman Lamor, age 47. |

## SLAVE SALES

| Date | Seller Last Name | Seller First Name | Buyer Last Name | Buyer First Name | Price | Transaction |
|------|------|------|------|------|------|------|
| 1807 | Amos | Mordicai | Amos | Shanta & Sarah | 140 pounds | Negro women Hager; 2 old horsess, 1 old wagon, 2 beds, 5 cattle, 9 hogs, 12 sheep, 2 chairs, tea kettle, hoes, axes, mattocks, grain sown in fields, 2 pr. Chanes. " The sum of forty pounds current money to me in hand payed beside the sum of fifty pounds current money settled with each of my Daughters for ten years work each as hired hands which make in hole the sum of one hundred and fortey pounds to me paid and settled by Shantaty and Sarah Amos....." |
| 1808 | Gray | Thomas H. | Barnes | John | $65.00 | One Negro girl, Mint, age 19. |
| 1808 | Mitchell | Eleanor | Mitchell | Mary | $100.00 | One Negro girl, Eliza, age 3. |
| 1808 | Preston | Benjamin | Street | John | 50 pounds, c.m. | One Negro man, Ben. |
| 1808 | Thompson | Alf | Anderson | Ann | 65 ponds, c.m. | Service of Negro Ruth & dau. Kise until they are age 31. |
| 1808 | Thompson | Alf | Poteet | Thomas | $100.00 | Service of Dinah until age 31, thereafter to be free. |

65

# SLAVE SALES

| Date | Seller Last Name | Seller First Name | Buyer Last Name | Buyer First Name | Price | Transaction |
|------|------------------|-------------------|-----------------|------------------|-------|-------------|
| 1810 | Bond | Mary | Adam | Negro | $100.00 | Hannah and her childred: Bill, Johathan, & Mary Ann. |
| 1811 | Cunningham | Cristin | Forwood | John | 15:00:00 | Negro Judy-24 & her child John Nelson, age 2. |
| 1811 | Stokes | Joseph | Wheeler | John F.R. | 500 pounds | Negro boys: Peter, Jacob, Abe and James. |
| 1811 | McComas | Daniel | Calwell | William | $36.00 | One Negro girl, Susanna, age 16. |
| 1811 | Cooper | Henry | Greenfield | Mary L. | Love & aff. | One Negro girl named Sal, age 8. Buyer also Janet C. Greenfield 1 dollar. |
| 1811 | Bond | Jacob | Hile | Thomas | $220.00 | A Negro woman named Dinah. |
| 1811 | Prigg | Edward | Worthington | William | 40 pounds | Service of Negro Cassandra for 5 years, thereafter she is to be manumitted and set free. |
| 1812 | Gorrel | John | Whitaker | Platt | $150.00 U.S. | One Negro slave, Cloe, age 8. |
| 1813 | Guyton | Joshua | Woolfolk- Balt City | Austin | $900 | Negroes Rachael-40, Ned-12, John-5, Tom-8, Rachael-8, Sue-3. |
| 1813 | Cooper | Henry | Archer | T.:R.,J. &S. | $300.00 | Services of Negro Mat or Nat for a period of 12 years. |

66

## SLAVE SALES

| Date | Seller Last Name | Seller First Name | Buyer Last Name | Buyer First Name | Price | Transaction |
|---|---|---|---|---|---|---|
| 1814 | Bennett | Phillip | Bennett | Henry | $2000.00 | Negroes Juliana-7 & Oelia-9; Also, livestock and household and farm furniture and goods. |
| 1814 | Smith | Paca | Giles | Cordelia | $1000.00 | Negro man Cline, boy Jacob and a girl Sarah. |
| 1814 | Murphy | John | Hall | George W. | $250.00 | Negro slave named Hannah. |
| 1814 | McComas | James | Dorney | Thomas | One dollar | One Negro man, Daniel. |
| 1814 | Hitchcock | Israel | Jarrett | Abraham | $200.00 | Negro girl & her children: Sidny & Dick. |
| 1814 | Foard | William | Watters | William | $600.00 | Negro man Charles and Yellow man Jack. |
| 1814 | Bolster | William | McComas | James | $600.00 | Negro man Daniel & Samson; also, one half part of a 40 ton schooner "William of Baltimore". |
| 1814 | Archer Estate | John | Green | Henretta | $116.62 | John Archer Estate with Thomas, Robert & Stevenson Archer as beneficiaries. |
| 1814 | Cowan | Roger B. | Henderson | George | 5 shillings | Negroes: James-60, Charlotte-30, Sal-27, Ann-25, Jacov-17, Michael-18, Matilda-9, harriot-7, Frank-5, Bill-18 mo. & Charles 10 months. |

67

# SLAVE SALES

| Date | Seller Last Name | Seller First Name | Buyer Last Name | Buyer First Name | Price | Transaction |
|------|------------------|-------------------|-----------------|------------------|-------|-------------|
| 1815 | Nelson | John | | Negro Jenny | $80.00 | One Negro girl, Hetty, age 6. |
| 1815 | Amos | Robert Jr. | Amos of B.C. | Isaac | $500.00 | One Negro man named Stephen. |
| 1815 | Hopkins | Rich & Frances | Hopkins-Black | Children of Frances | Love & affect- $1 | Following slaves: Hagar-34, Harriot-13, Emely-11, Charles-9, and Maria-7. |
| 1816 | Slade | Josias | Guyton | Benjamin | $300.00 | One mulatto woman Harriot, age 17. |
| 1816 | Carroll | Benjamin | Spicer | John | $44.00 | Services of Negro Jonas-19 for one year. |
| 1816 | Carroll | Benjamin | Jellott - B. C. | John | $400.00 | Negro Jacob Spencer age 28. |
| 1816 | Obrein | Charles | Watters | John | $470.00 | Negro girls Sarah- & Ann-4; Bay mare-4, 1 cow, 4 sheep, and sundry household furniture. |
| 1816 | Obrein | Charles | Watters | John | $500.00 | Negro James to be hired out until he earns $500.00 mortgage. |
| 1816 | Oneil | Owen | Onei - Was. DC | Bernard | $100.00 | Negro named Jim, age 25. |
| 1816 | Sewall | Charles | Carroll | Benjamin | $248.00 | Negroes James Spencer & Jacob Spencer. |
| 1816 | Beaty | James | Demos | John | $735.00 | Negro Frank 25; Also: 3 horses & harnesses, wagon, walnut chest, poplar chest, a feather bed w/furniture. |

# SLAVE SALES

| Date | Seller Last Name | Seller First Name | Buyer Last Name | Buyer First Name | Price | Transaction |
|---|---|---|---|---|---|---|
| 1817 | Brady (Agent) | James | Cruz- New Orleans LA | Antonio | $360.00 | One Negro girl Maria Glover, age 18, sold south to New Orleans. |
| 1817 | Deaver | Richard | Murphy | John | $275.00 | Female Negro Darkey & her children: Miranda, Milkah, & Metilda until each arrives at the age of 35. |
| 1818 | Moon-agent-Geo Woolsey | Jason | Chambers-Repeda Parish, LA. | William | $1000.00 | Negro girls Milkey-23 and Grace-20 sold south to Repeda Parish, Louisiana. |
| 1818 | Hall | Wm. & Edw | Dallam | Richard | $324:09:00 | Purchased in 1804 by Parker Hall. |
| 1818 | Richardson | William | Manefee -Tenn. | James | $717.50 | Negro woman Charlotte-22 and her child Hamer-2 child sold south to Davidson CountyTenn. |
| 1818 | Richardson | Robert | Rains- Tenn. | John | $500.00 | One Negro boy Sam-14 sold south th Davidson Co, Tenn. |
| 1818 | Norris | Silas | Norris | Rhesa | $175.00 | Services of Negro boy Sam until 1838, 20 years. |
| 1818 | Nabb - Balt Cty | John | Shekell | Lavine & Julia | $225.00 | One Negro girl, Harriot-14. |
| 1818 | Nabb-Balt City | John | Shekell, Nieces | Lavine & Julia | Love & affect | One Negro boy Daniel-7 & girl Emiline-4. |

## SLAVE SALES

| Date | Seller Last Name | Seller First Name | Buyer Last Name | Buyer First Name | Price | Transaction |
|------|------|------|------|------|------|------|
| 1818 | Johnson | Moses | Wheeler | Ann | $215.00 | Negro women Phillis and her children: Mary, George. One wagon, one bay horse, one gray mare, and sorrel colt. |
| 1818 | Guyton | Benjamin | Manefee- Tenn | James | $900.00 | Sold south to Davidson County Tennessee: Mulatto women Hetty-30 & son Stephen-12. |
| 1818 | Butler | Lewis | Menefee- Tenn | James N. | $645.00 | Negro slave Isaac-21 sold south to Davison County Tennessee. |
| 1818 | Evans Cecil Co | James | Woolfolk- Balt City | Austin | $225.00 | Negro girl named Sarah-18. |
| 1818 | Brown | William | Woolfolk- Georgia | Austin | $600.00 | Negro Tom-27 sold to Austin Woolford and transportrd to Augusta County, Georgia. |
| 1818 | Brierly | William | Chambers | William | $300.00 | One Negro slave, Milly, age 15. |
| 1818 | Kelly | James | Michael | Jacob | $400.00 | Negro boy Jonas 25. |
| 1819 | Hays | Archer | Hays | Archer | $100.00 | One sixth share in Negro Manuel & Violet & her child. |

# SLAVE SALES

| Date | Seller Last Name | Seller First Name | Buyer Last Name | Buyer First Name | Price | Transaction |
|---|---|---|---|---|---|---|
| 1819 | Mithchell | Sarah | Nolan- Georgia | John | $700.00 | Negro woman Maria-23 & her children, Harriot-4, Ann-18 mos. Sold South to Georgia. |
| 1819 | Osborn | Cyrus | Nolan- Georgia | John | $1400.00 | Two slaves Simon-38, Vince 18 sold South to Georgia. |
| 1819 | Pressbury | George | Herbert | James | $200.00 | Services of Negro David-7 until 1/1/1842. |
| 1819 | Presbury | George | Nolan- Georgia | John | $300.00 | One Negro slave named Tom. |
| 1819 | Presbury | George | Parker | Samuel | $500.00 | One Negro man Tom. |
| 1819 | Vandergraft | John | Mitchell | Sarah | $150.00 | One Negro boy named Hampton. |
| 1819 | Johnson | Moses | Nolan- Georgia | John | $600. | Negro Phil age 26 sold South to Georgia. |
| 1819 | Gover | Robert | Grafton | Nathan | $300.00 | Negro girl Ann 10 and her infant child. |
| 1819 | Robinson | William | Dorsey | Jam | $37.76 | Services of Negro Sophia until she is set free at 35. |
| 1819 | Hitchcock | Isaac | Ayers Sr. | Thomas | $128.00 | Negro slave named York, age 37. |
| 1819 | Hawkins | Mary | Mitchell | Sarah | $190.00 | One Negro girl Sarah. |

71

# SLAVE SALES

| Date | Seller Last Name | Seller First Name | Buyer Last Name | Buyer First Name | Price | Transaction |
|---|---|---|---|---|---|---|
| 1819 | Green | Clement | Nichols- Tenn. | John | $370.00 | One Negro boy Bob, age 13 sold south to Davidson County Tenn. |
| 1819 | Donahue | John | Noland- Geogia | John | $700.00 | Negro slave, Hampton-25 sold south to Wilks County Georgia. |
| 1819 | Chauncy | Elizabeth | Gilbert Balt. C. | Harry | $400.00 | Negro slave Sarah-17. |
| 1819 | Brownley | James | Murphy | John | $788.31 | One Negro David, 3 horses, 1 cow, 8 sheep, 14 hogs, and sundry household goods. |
| 1819 | Bond | Thomas W. | Chauncy | George | $500.00 | Negroes Stokes-43 and Stansbury-16. |
| 1819 | Ady | Solomon | Nolan- Georgia | John | $650.00 | One Negro slave Jacob-17 sold south to Wilks County Georgia. |
| 1819 | Jarrett | Abraham | Nolan- Georgia | John | $825.00 | Two Negro boys Stephen-13 and John-11 sold South to Georgia. |
| 1819 | Griffith | Edward | Noland- Georgia | John | $700.00 | One Negro slave Joe. |
| 1820 | Bayles | John | Rumsey | Charles | $275.00 | One Negro girl Violey-15. |
| 1820 | Wheeler | James | Bradford | Samuel | $100.00 | Mortgage for one Negro boy Jacob. |
| 1820 | Quinlan | Benjamin | Clark | William | $600.00 | Negro Sarah & children: Ned, Sophia, Joan. |

## SLAVE SALES

| Date | Seller Last Name | Seller First Name | Buyer Last Name | Buyer First Name | Price | Transaction |
|---|---|---|---|---|---|---|
| 1820 | Mathews | Josiah | Osborn | William | $1000.00 | Negroes:Dinah,Charles,Henry.Also gray horse, bay horse, brown horse, oxen & Cart, 2 milk cows & calves. |
| 1820 | Hughes | Zenus | Mason-Balt Cty. | Peter | $245.00 | Negro girl, Milly-12. |
| 1820 | Galloway | Barthia | Galloway Children | Aquill's | Love & affect | Negroes: Abram, Sam, Hazzard, Phillip, Jim & Harlot. |
| 1820 | Bond | Buckler | Howard | Rebecca | 1 dollar | One slave called Hester. |
| 1820 | Bayles | John | Rumsey | Charles | $400.00 | One Negro Wilks-20. |
| 1820 | Ady | Chloe | Ady | Chloe | love & affect | Negro Rachael-26 & her ch: Jacob-2, Mary-4 months. |
| 1820 | Forwood | John | Gandy | Uriah | $400.00 | Negro man Nance-24. |
| 1821 | Sappington | Richardson | Malone- Alabama | Robert | $245.00 | Negro woman Jenny-22 sold South to Alabama. |
| 1821 | Cain | Elizabeth | Dorsey | Henry | $100.00 | Negro girl Elizabeth called Sis. |
| 1821 | Ady | Chloe | Ady-dau | Chloe | $5 shillings | Negro girl Sarah-6 to serve until the age of 34. |
| 1821 | Ashmore | John | Oldfield | Robert | $800.00 | Negroes Nat and Charles. |

73

# SLAVE SALES

| Date | Seller Last Name | Seller First Name | Buyer Last Name | Buyer First Name | Price | Transaction |
|------|------------------|-------------------|-----------------|------------------|-------|-------------|
| 1821 | Birchhead | Elizabeth | Asewall | Charles | $300.00 | Negro Gibson-19. |
| 1821 | Bond | Thomas | Bond | James | $200.00 | Negro Isaac-16. |
| 1821 | Bussey | Elizabeth | Williams- LA | Archibald | $275.00 | Negro girl Harriot-16. |
| 1821 | Ruff | John | Nelson | John | $500.00 | Negro boy Frank-13 7 girl Ann-17. |
| 1821 | Webster | Sam'l Lee | Hall | Aquilla | $400.00 | Negro Rachael and children: Jacob, Mary. |
| 1821 | Dallam | Henretta | Paca Blandy | Frances | $5.00 | Service of Negro Robert until age 30. |
| 1821 | Richardson | Samuel | Richardson | William | $400.00 | One Negro slave Sam age 38. |
| 1821 | Richardson | Samuel | Richardson | William | $400.00 | One Negro slave Peter age 18. |
| 1821 | Mitchell | Sarah | Malone-Alabama | Robert | $200.00 | Negro girl Sarah-12 sold South to Alabama. |
| 1821 | McGaw | John | Williams- LA | Archibald | $160.00 | One Negro boy Isaac-8. |
| 1821 | Mathews | Josiah | Williams- LA | Archibald | $1550.00 | Negro Dinah & infant. Girls:Hariot,Charlotte; Boys: William, Lew, Chas, Henry. |
| 1821 | Mcates | Henry | Malone- Alabama | Robert | $325.00 | Negroes John-10 and David-9 sold South to Alabama. |

74

## SLAVE SALES

| Date | Seller Last Name | Seller First Name | Buyer Last Name | Buyer First Name | Price | Transaction |
|------|------------------|-------------------|-----------------|------------------|-------|-------------|
| 1821 | Hollis | William | Day | Ch.of Sarah | $300.00 | Negroes Ellen, Candy and Charles. |
| 1821 | Hill | Aaron | Ady | James | $200.00 | Negro boy Spencer & girl Charlotte; Also goods, stock, etc. |
| 1821 | Guyton | Jane | Anderson-Kentucky | David | $300.00 | Negro girl Jenny-19 sold South to Kentucky. |
| 1821 | Smith | Winston | Smith | Jacob | $1000.00 | Negroes:Dinah, Dick, Jacob, Ben; Also, livestock, farm equip. & household furniture. |
| 1822 | McClaskey | William | King- Balt Cty | John | $275.00 | One Negro boy named Phillip-10. |
| 1822 | Kennard | Matthew | Jarvis | John | 12:00:00 | Negro Sall-22 and her ch: Harriot -4 & George 1 1/2, 2 cows. |
| 1822 | Kennard | Isaac | King - B.C. | John | $525.00 | Sarah's child Simon 15 mos. |
| 1822 | Kenney Sr. | John | Woolfolk- Balt City | Austin | $350.00 | Negro women Maria & her child Hanna-18 mos. |
| 1822 | Kenney | John | Woolfolk- Balt Cty | Austin | $350 | Negro woman Maria-17 & her child Hanna-18 mo. |
| 1822 | Knight | James | Oldhan Cecil Co | Chas | $335.00 | Mullato boy named Alexander-17. |

75

## SLAVE SALES

| Date | Seller Last Name | Seller First Name | Buyer Last Name | Buyer First Name | Price | Transaction |
|------|------------------|-------------------|-----------------|------------------|-------|-------------|
| 1822 | Lee | William O. | Dorsey | Col. Henry | $500.00 | Negro William age 19. |
| 1822 | Morgan | James Lee | Green B.C. | Richard | $400.00 | Negro man John purchased from Edward Prigg. |
| 1822 | Nelson | Aquilla | Woolfolk- Balt.Cty. | R.T. | $850.00 | Two Negroes Abram-19 & Jacob-20. |
| 1822 | Perryman | Isaac | Snowden | Thos | $400.00 | One Negro boy-Evan-18 -Sold to AA County. |
| 1822 | Richardson | William | Landale | William | $390.00 | Negro Lad Peter-12. |
| 1822 | Scharf | Edmund T. | Scharf | Rebecca | Love & affect. | One Negro Paisha-18; Also: 3 feather beds, chest, 2 template stoves, 1 weaver loom, trunk, 2 tables & 6 tea spoons (silver, 2 iron pots, Dutch oven, set carpenter tools, and crops growing in the fields. |
| 1822 | Johnson | Moses | Green of Balt | Richard | $240 | Negro girls Mary-12 and Jusy Ann-12 |
| 1822 | Wilson | Isaac | Woolfolk- Balt City. | Austin | $640.00 | One yellow slave Abraham-15 & one girl Rosetta-15. |
| 1822 | Kean | John | Cain | Elizabeth | $135 | Negro Lyttle to serve until he is 30 yrs old. |

76

## SLAVE SALES

| Date | Seller Last Name | Seller First Name | Buyer Last Name | Buyer First Name | Price | Transaction |
|------|------------------|-------------------|-----------------|------------------|-------|-------------|
| 1822 | Watters | Stephen | Ely | Matilda | $30.00 | One Negro slave Mary Ann-10 mon. old. |
| 1822 | Dulaney | Joseph | Murphy | John | $491.68 | Negro Harriot-20 to serve until 26;Sam-3, Harrit-2 Also, livestock and sundry goods. |
| 1822 | Kennard | Isaac | Bond | Thomas | $3844 | Assumed debt of $3844 owed by Hanna Lee. "All the stock, household stuff, furniture, imp and all crops growing in the field" Negores Harriot-20, and her child 3 mon., Lavine-3,Isabella-1, Joshua-13, Nat-3, Harry-8, Joseph-6 |
| 1822 | Johnson | Josiah | Harding of Tenn | David | $700 | Negro boy Mike-18 & girl Hanner-16 |
| 1822 | Clark | William | Harding- Tenn. | David | $400.00 | Negro slave Benjamin age 22 sold South to Tennessee. |
| 1822 | Davis | Elijah | Woolfolk- Balt City | Austin | $475.00 | Negro boy called Pinkey, age 17. |
| 1822 | Davis | James | Anderson-Kentucky | David | $250.00 | Negro girl Jenny, age 15 sold South to Kentucky. |
| 1822 | Dorsey | Henry | Woolfolk- Balt Cty | Austin | $800.00 | Negro Stephen-23 and Martin-17. |
| 1822 | Ayers | Thomas W. | Ayers,Sr. | Thomas | $300.00 | Negro called Samuel age 18. |

77

## SLAVE SALES

| Date | Seller Last Name | Seller First Name | Buyer Last Name | Buyer First Name | Price | Transaction |
|------|------------------|-------------------|-----------------|------------------|-------|-------------|
| 1822 | Ellis | Jamina | Guyton | Joshua | $216.00 | Negro girl Mary age 15. |
| 1822 | Ely | John | Hallowell-Kentucky | Irwin | $277.00 | Negro woman Fanny, age 22. |
| 1822 | Gallion | Jacob | Michael | Ethan | $149.62 | Negro Susan-24 and child Frances-3. |
| 1822 | Gover | Robert | Prigg | Edward | $645.00 | Negro lads Edward and George, boy Robert-15. |
| 1822 | Hall | Edward | Woolfolk- Balt Cty | R.T. | $1262.00 | Negroes John-28, Bob-23, and Winston-20. |
| 1822 | Henderson | George | Woolfolk- Balt Cty | R.T. | $335.00 | Negro slave Bob-33. |
| 1822 | Hitchcock | Asael | Hitchcock | Charles | $580 | Negroes Harriot-15, Lucy-14 and Benjamin -12. |
| 1822 | Allender | Nicholas | Silver | William | $190.00 | Negro girl Rachael age 11. |
| 1822 | Deaver | Aquila | Hall | Edward | $1316.66 | Negroes:Rachael-35, Gideon-8, Goldsmith-18, Milkey-12, Nat Bradford-32, Bill Moulton-23, Jacob-10 and Daniel-8. |

78

## SLAVE SALES

| Date | Seller Last Name | Seller First Name | Buyer Last Name | Buyer First Name | Price | Transaction |
|------|------------------|-------------------|-----------------|------------------|-------|-------------|
| 1823 | Griffin | Thomas | Cherbonnier | Peter | $350.00 | Negro Harriet & Children:Sarah, Henretta, & Caroline. |
| 1823 | Silver | Benjamin | Morgan | Frances | one dollar | The buyer, Frances Morgan, was the seller, Benjamin Silver's, step-daughter. |
| 1823 | Johnson | Moses | Woolfolk- Balt City | Austin | $230.00 | Negro Phebe & her manchild Jacob-2. |
| 1823 | Lee | James | Woolfolk- Balt City | Austin | $350. | Mulatto Abram-20 (yellow complection and hair). |
| 1823 | Grupy | Frances | Baker | Sarah | $355.00 | Negro Susan and manchild John-18 months. |
| 1823 | Enlows | James | Kennedy | James | $200.00 | Negro man Elisha, 1 bed, 1 stove, 2 looms & tackling. |
| 1823 | Dallam | Henretta | Dallam | Thos. | Love & affect | Services of Frisby & Amos until they are freed at 30. |
| 1823 | Dallam | Henretta | Dallam | Jas. | Love & affect | Services of Horace &Henry until freed at age 30. |
| 1823 | Bateman | Sarah | Birchead | Samuel | $250.00 | Negro slave George-17. |
| 1823 | Allen | Richard | Woolfolk- Tenn. | Joseph | $305.00 | Negro man Edward-24 sold south to Jackson County Tennessee. |

79

# SLAVE SALES

| Date | Seller Last Name | Seller First Name | Buyer Last Name | Buyer First Name | Price | Transaction |
|---|---|---|---|---|---|---|
| 1823 | Carlile- Balt.CO. | David | Kennedy | James | $500.00 | Negroes Elizabeth-20 and Harry-18. |
| 1824 | Maulsby | Israel | Richardson | William | $150.00 | One Negro girl Eleanor-11. |
| 1824 | Wilson | Thomas | Mathews | John | $92.50 | Negro willed to Ann Hanson by her Uncle Ben. Mathews. |
| 1824 | White- Cecil Co. | Thos | Woolfolk- Balt Cty | Austin | $600.00 | Negro Samuel-20 and Jacob-11. |
| 1824 | Ruff | Henry | Nelson | Aquila | $53.82 | One Negro girl, Ellen-11. |
| 1824 | Richardson | William | Stumo | Thomas | $90.00 | One Negro girl, Eleanore-11. |
| 1824 | Michael | Naomi | Michael | Susanna | not given | Phoebe-40, Dinah-18 and Philip-3. |
| 1824 | Jarrett | Abraham | Jones | Benjamin | $40.00 | Services of Negro women Teney until July 1, 1828. |
| 1824 | Hanson Kent Co | James | Rice | Abe | $870.00 | Negroes purchased at following prices: Hester- $20. Sharlot-$250., Harriot-$250., Rachael-$200., Ann- $150. |
| 1824 | Gilbert | Abner | Guyton | Ed. & John | $125.00 | One Negro boy Jarrett-17. |

# SLAVE SALES

| Date | Seller Last Name | Seller First Name | Buyer Last Name | Buyer First Name | Price | Transaction |
|------|------------------|-------------------|-----------------|------------------|-------|-------------|
| 1824 | Baily | Benedict | Bailey | Aeil | $375.00 | Negro women Dinah, s feather beds, 1 cupboard, chest, 3 tables, 2 laddles, 7silver teaspoons, set knives & forks, 6 T. spoons, 3 wheels, bay horse, mare & colt yoke oxen, 9 cattle, 20 sheep, 13 hogs,3 ploughs, 1 harrow, king mellt & 3 wegges, 2 corn hoes, cart,2 pitchforks,set carpenter & joiners tools, ax,2 kittles, 2 iron pots, & racks, set crockery ware,set tubs & pales, set cider casks, 1 mattock, 4 guns, 8 cheers, fire shovel & tongs, looking glass, desk, 2 iron tea kittles, check reels, plow geers. Sold South to Tennessee |
| 1824 | Johnson | Thos & M | Stump | Thomas | $90.00 | One mulatto boy, Bill, six years old. |
| 1824 | Galloway | Moses& Wm. | Hoke | Peter | $156.952 | Yellow girl named Harriet, 3 sorel mare & colt, 3 cows, template stove, 5 beds, mahogany sec. Desk & dinning table, wool yarn, 6 windsor chairs, pr. Anirons, 7 hogs. |
| 1825 | McComas | Aquila | Chabart- LA | L. | $300.00 | One Negro slave Isaac sold South to Louisiana. |
| 1825 | Poteet | James | Poteet | John | $1200.00 | Negroes: Lisa-15, Gabriel-12,Ann-10, Harry-8, Bob-6 and Quil-4; Also livestock & house & farm equip. |

81

## SLAVE SALES

| Date | Seller Last Name | Seller First Name | Buyer Last Name | Buyer First Name | Price | Transaction |
|------|------------------|-------------------|-----------------|------------------|-------|-------------|
| 1825 | Mitchell | Sarah | Chabart- LA | L. | $320.00 | Negro woman Hanna-35, Hamp-9, and girl Mint-5. sold South to Luisanna |
| 1825 | Mccatee | Henry | Richardson | Wm. | $500.00 | Negro Milly-18, 5 horses, 2 wagons, yoke oxen, cart. |
| 1825 | Lee | Richard | Reynolds | Sam | $275.00 | Hannah-17 & her manchild Charles-2 mos. Old |
| 1825 | Hall | Edward | Henderson | George | $300.00 | One Negro boy Mike-age 30. |
| 1825 | Butler | Clement | Woolfolk- BaltCity | R.T | $275.00 | One yellow girl Louisa, age 16. |
| 1825 | Bayless | John | Timmons | Edward | $135.00 | One Negro man George-40. |
| 1825 | Almony  Balt.Co. | Wm. | Mullen- Miss. | Theo B | $115.00 | Negro Margaret-35 sold South to Monroe County Mississippi. |
| 1825 | Kean | John | Chabart- LA | L. | $450.00 | Sold south to Louisana Negro girls: Bet-17, Margaret-12, Lucy-10. |
| 1825 | Miller | William F. | Bayless | Jephamiah | $200.00 | One Negro boy Jarrett-10 until he becomes 35 yrs. Old. |
| 1826 | Gladden | John | Gladden | James | $300.00 | Negro Rachael and her child Grace. |

82

## SLAVE SALES

| Date | Seller Last Name | Seller First Name | Buyer Last Name | Buyer First Name | Price | Transaction |
|------|------------------|-------------------|-----------------|------------------|-------|-------------|
| 1826 | Picking-Balt Cty | Jas. | Downey | Thomas | $100.00 | One Negro man named Perry. |
| 1826 | Norris | Rhess | Greenfield | Henry | $150.00 | Negro Sara-23, bay mare-6, bay horse-10, colt-2. |
| 1826 | Greenfield | Henry | Thompson | Edward | $97.00 | Negro Hannah age 45. |
| 1826 | Brown | Mary B. | Kelso | John | $175.00 | Yellow women Phillis for 2 yrs. And Philip to serve until he is 28 yrs old. |
| 1826 | James | Sarah | Richardson | Wm. & Rob't | Adm. Est. | Negro Charlotte-25 and Jacob-4, one eight day clock. |
| 1827 | Hall | Josias | Semmond-dau | Martha | One cent | One Negro girl named Polly-14. |
| 1827 | Wilson | Rachael | Miller | Horatio | $60.00 | Negro Rebecca for 18 yrs. & Manuella for 29 years. |
| 1827 | Wilson | William | Webster | John | $200.00 | Negro Lewis-13 to serve until 1850, Emerson-9 until 1856. |
| 1827 | Shell | Wm. | Billingslea | Barnett | $150.00 | Negro Jacob who is now abscounded & run-a-way. |
| 1827 | Henderson | Frances | Holland | Robert W. | $100.00 | Service of Negro Esau-30 for a period of 5 yrs. |

# SLAVE SALES

| Date | Seller Last Name | Seller First Name | Buyer Last Name | Buyer First Name | Price | Transaction |
|---|---|---|---|---|---|---|
| 1827 | Hall | George W. | Hall | Sarah | $600.00 | Negro , girl Ellen, girl Eliza; Sundry household goods. |
| 1827 | Herbert | James | Woolfolk- Balt City | Austin | $300.00 | Mulatto Charlott-18 & her manchild Jarrett-18 mos. |
| 1827 | Jarrett | Abraham | Bull | Elisha | $200.00 | Negro Jack-14 for a term of 16 years. |
| 1828 | Johnson | Thomas | Woolfolk- Balt City | R.T. | $405.00 | One Negro slave Abrham-18. |
| 1828 | Smith | Henry | Woolfolk- Balt City | Austin | $300.00 | Negro boy Joshua age 15. |
| 1828 | Presbury | William | Watters | Rachel | $150.00 | Negro Abraham-22. |
| 1828 | Hall | Josias | Lemmon | Martha | One cent | Mulatto boy Peter age 14. |
| 1828 | Greme | Augustus | Woolfolk- Balt City | Austin | $340.00 | Negro man named Jerry. |
| 1828 | Brown | Mary | Brown | Geo. Edw. Thos | Love & $5.00 | Negroes: Wat 18, Nick 12, John 8, Jack 8, Charles 6 and Naomi 10. |
| 1828 | Bond | F.C.& N. | Howard | Mary Ann | $225.00 | One Negro man Jack age 35. |
| 1828 | Caroline | Frances | Howard | Francis | $150.00 debt | One Negro girl Milly age 13. |

84

# SLAVE SALES

| Date | Seller Last Name | Seller First Name | Buyer Last Name | Buyer First Name | Price | Transaction |
|------|------------------|-------------------|-----------------|------------------|-------|-------------|
| 1828 | Amos | James B. | Chabert- LA | Leon | $500.00 | Negro Charlotte-30, George-10, John-8, Isaac-5 and Ester-4 sold South to Louisanna. |
| 1828 | Allender | Nicholas | Hatchen | Joshua | $186.44 | Negro girl Maria. |
| 1828 | Robinson | Joseph | Woolfolk- Balt City | Austin | $300.00 | Negro boy Joshua age 15. |
| 1829 | Hays | Nathan & Thos | Norris | Luther | $545.84 | 1828 mortgage, Negroes Parker-18, Louis-16, Tom-11, Eliza-17, Dinah-17 and Betsy-5. |
| 1829 | Norris | Luther | Macbeth-Del | L. & Wm | $700.00 | Negroes Parker-28 and Louis-18. |
| 1829 | Saunders | Joseph | Bottom | Robert | $50.00 | Service of Negro Grace for 4 years beginning 7/18/1929. |
| 1830 | Galloway | Abraham | Kelso-Balt. Cty | George | $200.00 | One Negro Alexander age 27. |
| 1830 | Rean | John | Woolfolk- Balt City | Austin | $1400 | Sold by John Ran, sheriff property of James Wallace- Negroes: Jacob14, Mosese-11, Dinah-13,Harriet-4, Phillis-40,Phebe-5,Milky-12,Prina-30 and Eliza-8 mo. |
| 1830 | Lytle | Rachael | Gittings-B. Co. | Dr. David | $161 | Services of Negro Bill until freed on 1/1938. |

# SLAVE SALES

| Date | Seller Last Name | Seller First Name | Buyer Last Name | Buyer First Name | Price | Transaction |
|---|---|---|---|---|---|---|
| 1830 | Kean | Joan | Kelso, Balt. City | Geoge | $300 | One Negro boy Cato. |
| 1830 | Jarrett, Jr. | Jesse | Jarrett | Luther | $100 | My half of Negro Luke, age 18 |
| 1830 | Wetherall | James | Dorsey | Thomas | $125 | Negro George-6 and sundry goods. |
| 1830 | Coale | Elizabeth | Gilbert | Elizabeth | $87.60 | Negroes Charles-12, Eliza-10, Moses-8, Rachael-5 and lawson-3; All to be free at age 38. |
| 1830 | Brown | William | Willis | William R. | $100.00 | Services of Maria, 25 until freed on 9/15/1840. |
| 1830 | Bond | James T. | Woolfolk- Balt City | Austin | $300.00 | One Negro slave Isaac Brown, age 19. |
| 1830 | Baxter | Benjamin | Allender | George | Debt. Pd. | One Negro boy Henry age 12. |
| 1830 | Huge | Samuel | Kelso-Balt. City | George | $200 | One Negro girl Sarah, age 17. |
| 1830 | Henderson | Joseph | Henderson | Thomas | $200.00 | Negro family 21 7 ch; Susanna-3 and Cate-1; All to be free at age 38. |
| 1831 | Renshaw | Otho | Amos | William | $125 | Negroes Tim-11, Rose-8, Henry-5, Deby-2, Sundry goods. |

86

# SLAVE SALES

| Date | Seller Last Name | Seller First Name | Buyer Last Name | Buyer First Name | Price | Transaction |
|---|---|---|---|---|---|---|
| 1831 | Wetherall | James | Norris | Capt. Otho | $200 | Birkhead estate; Negro Abrahm's services until 1838 when he is to be freed. |
| 1831 | Scott | Otho | Preston- a Black Man | Harry | $1 | Negroes Caroline-26, Merilon-2, and Sarah-1; All to be free at the age of 26. |
| 1831 | Renshaw | Elizabeth | Whitaker | Joshua | $245 | Negro Eliza and her manchild George. |
| 1831 | Glasglow | Elizabeth | Norris | Cornelia | $126.50 | James Pannell, Adm., Negro Rose 12- to be manumitted at age of 25. |
| 1831 | Botts | James | Botts | John | $500 | Negro Tillie-31, Joshua-9, Dennis-7, and a girl 3. |
| 1831 | McComas | Aquila | McComas | Mary Ann | $300 | Negro Rachael and boy Phil. |
| 1831 | Hollis | Benjamin | Pollard, Balt City | George | 73.45 | Negro Jim, Rachael, boy Gilbert, girl Harriet, yoke of oxen & cart, 6 horses, 13 cows. |
| 1831 | Wetherall | Sarah | McComas | Harriet | $5 | Negro slave William Henry, age 3. |
| 1831 | Renshaw | Elizabeth | Renshaw | Thomas | $284 | Negroes John and Milky; one cow, one horse. |
| 1832 | Cole | Sarah | Cole | James | $250 | Mulatto boys: Jacob -18, Jim-22, Negro Polly-14. |

# SLAVE SALES

| Date | Seller Last Name | Seller First Name | Buyer Last Name | Buyer First Name | Price | Transaction |
|------|------------------|-------------------|-----------------|------------------|-------|-------------|
| 1832 | Stump | Cassandra | Hawkins-Negro Cecil Co | Eliz | $5- | Assign Negro girl Sarah to her until she becomes free at 18. |
| 1832 | Norris-Balt City | Wm | Hollis | Richard | $100 | One Negro girl Betsy-10. |
| 1832 | Boyd | Cooper | Wheeler | Hercules | $75 | One Negro slave Amarilla Wheeler. |
| 1832 | Renshaw | Elizabeth | Hanway | Washington | $120 | Negro Eliz. Sutton-16 and her infant Julie Sutton: Elizabeth to serve until 1844, Julie until 1860 (til 28). |
| 1833 | Garrerrson, Balt Co | Mary | Denneson-Free woman of color | Margaret | $30 | John Dennison, her husband. |
| 1833 | Grafton | Martin | Harkins | Joseph | $25 | James Wetherall, Estate;Negro Nelly-20 to serve until 35, no longer. |
| 1833 | Wilson | Joshua | Pitcock | Benjamin | $160 | Negro Nancy to serve 11 years and then be free. |
| 1834 | Troup | Eliza | Smith-Colored | Isaac | $100 | Negro slave Milcha, age 8 yrs, 11 mo. |
| 1834 | Gorsuch | Charles | Balt City | Negro Sarah | $20 | Negro Mary-8, to be manumitted & free at age of 18. |
| 1834 | Dorsey | Archibald | Crook, Balt City | Wm | $113.08 | Mulattoes Nick-24 & LJyod-22 to be held as security for the payment of said note. |

# SLAVE SALES

| Date | Seller Last Name | Seller First Name | Buyer Last Name | Buyer First Name | Price | Transaction |
|------|------------------|-------------------|-----------------|------------------|-------|-------------|
| 1834 | Cooley | Sarah | Cooley | Daniel | $200 | My half of Negro Jim. |
| 1835 | Gover | Robert | Kennard-Slave | George | $100 | Balance due to pay for his freedom. |
| 1835 | Templin | Hannah | Worthington | William | Value Received | Negroes John, Margaret & Stephen. |
| 1835 | Bull | Elish & John | Amos | Daniel | $1 | One Negro woman named Phebe. |
| 1836 | Coale | Elizabeth | Prigg | Mark | $1 | Negro Fanny, age 34. |
| 1836 | Greenland | Elisha | Prigg | Mark | $25 | Negro children: Milly-3 and Sylvester-1. |
| 1836 | Kelly | Margaret | Stump | Susan | $50 | Negro girl Eliza-9 to serve until age 18. |
| 1836 | Mavates | Henry | Wheeler | Henry | $100 | Negro Ellen, age 45. |
| 1836 | Preston | Harry | Stephenson-Colored | Caroline | Love& aff | One colored lad America, son of Caroline. |
| 1836 | Stuaurt | Ephraim | McComas | John | $250 | Negro Jud-30 to serve until 38; Negro girls: Henryetta 6, Sarah 4 and Milcha 4-slaves for life. |

## SLAVE SALES

| Date | Seller Last Name | Seller First Name | Buyer Last Name | Buyer First Name | Price | Transaction |
|------|------------------|-------------------|-----------------|------------------|-------|-------------|
| 1836 | Thornburg | Joseph | Webster | Elizabeth | $4204 | Estate administrators: Patrick McCauley, John Latrobe, William Murray B. city; "Mt. Repose" property: Negroes men:Jacob, Tim, Frank, Dan Women: Sarah and Harriet "Spesutia" property: Men: Isaac, Asbury, Jacob, Ned, John, and Charles; Women: Hetty, Sarah, and Harriet Girls: Eliza, Rachael, Isabel, Juliet, Patience, maragaret, Charlotte and Susan. |
| 1836 | Wilson | Wm | Haynes-Colored | Joseph | $100 | Negro Dinah Haynes & all children she has had since 1827. |
| 1837 | Cholk | Ellen | Webster | Richard | $200 | Negro boys Hillary-8 and Daniel-5. |
| 1837 | Howlett | Elizabeth | Enfield | Jacob | $600 | One Negro slave called Bill. |
| 1837 | McComas | Mary | Bennett-Balt. Cty | John | $100 | One Negro girl Juliet. |
| 1838 | Ruff | Henry | Ruff | Daniel | $365 | Negro Ellen-23 until she is 28 years of age; Three Negro children: Edward, Hohn & Howie , slaves for life. |
| 1839 | Anderson | Benjamin | Dickey-D.C. | Edwin | $500 | Negro Isaac until he is 35 yrs of age. |

90

## SLAVE SALES

| Date | Seller Last Name | Seller First Name | Buyer Last Name | Buyer First Name | Price | Transaction |
|---|---|---|---|---|---|---|
| 1839 | Bussey | Henry | Bond- LA | Joshua | $450 | One Negro woman Sophy age 19, sold South to Louisana. |
| 1839 | McComas | Martha | Amos-Balt Cty | Dr. Corbin | $472 | Negroes Harry & Ellen-1 1/2' 1 cow, 2 sheep, sundries. |
| 1839 | Stump D.C. | Samuel | Hoke | Jacob | $492 | Negro Rachael-28 & her ch: Benj-3 & Margaret Ann-2. |
| 1840 | Amos | Joshua | Amos-Balt Cty | Dr. Corbin | $160 | One Negro woman named Gin. |
| 1840 | Gorsuch | Rezin & Susan | Mitchell | Richard | $5 | Negro Sarah and her ch: Lewis 7 Albert, livestock & goods. |
| 1840 | Shields-Negro | Averilla | Mitchell | Sylvester | $10 | "My son David –4- to serve until he is 21 yrs of age." |
| 1841 | Hall | Juliana | Chew | Washington | $1 | Negro girls Rachael-18 7 Henretta-8; Also livestock, carts, wagons, carriages and sulky. |
| 1841 | Lennan | Ann | Wheeler | Bennett | $5 | Negroes: Fanny, George, Henry, and Rosetta; Negro Zachariah to Hellen Bennett. |
| 1843 | Preston | Mary | Mitchell | John | $100 | Negro boy Wm. Henry Shields-6 until he is 21; crop of 20 acres oats, 1 piano, 2 feather beds. |

# SLAVE SALES

| Date | Seller Last Name | Seller First Name | Buyer Last Name | Buyer First Name | Price | Transaction |
|---|---|---|---|---|---|---|
| 1843 | Scott | Otho | Hall- Negro | Edward | $167 | One Negro woman Phebe and her child Jane. |
| 1843 | Dorsey | Dr. Archibald | McComas-Trustee | Elizabeth | $5 | Negro Charlotte & her ch: Henry, Wesley, & Charles - to be held in trust for my wife and Sarah her sister. |
| 1843 | Cathcart | William | Cathcart | George | $100 | Negro boy Robert until he is 21 yrs of age. One cow, 5 sheep, 6 horses, feather bed, corner cupboard. |
| 1843 | Whitlock | James | Archer | Parker | 4250.00 | Service of Negro Henry-19 for 9 years. |
| 1843 | Kean | Aquilla | Bayless, Wash Co | James | $300 | Negro Sarah-24. |
| 1844 | Griffith | John | Hill | Russell | $5.00 | One Negro women called Mary. |
| 1844 | Norris | Alexander | Bond-Colored | Charles | $100.00 | Negro Elizabeth-6 dau. Of Rose, to serve Charles Bond until she becomes 16 yrs. Old, then to be free. |
| 1845 | Pannell | James | Williams | James & Hanna | $99.00 | Services of Negro Charles-29 until set free on 4/10/1848. |
| 1845 | Thomas | Herman | Chambers | Eleanor | $650.00 | Negro boys:Thomas-17, Peter-17,George-9. |
| 1846 | Swartz | Wm & Ephraim | Swartz | Mary Ann | $150.00 | One Negro girl called Kit. |

92

# SLAVE SALES

| Date | Seller Last Name | Seller First Name | Buyer Last Name | Buyer First Name | Price | Transaction |
|---|---|---|---|---|---|---|
| 1846 | Boggs- Balt. Co | John & Alex | Glen | John | $1100.00 | Following Negroes: Michael, Ned, Titus, Jacob, Milly, and her five children. |
| 1846 | Walker | George | Coale- Negro | Daniel | $100.00 | One Negro women Caroline Billingsley. |
| 1846 | Coale Negro | Daniel | Billingsley- Neg. | Sam | $100.00 | One Negro women Caroline Billingsley. |
| 1846 | Gilbert | Elizabeth | Stephenson | James | $175.00 | Negro women Rachael and her daughter Milly. |
| 1846 | Stephenson | James | Stephenson | Hannah | $175.00 | Negro Rachael, and Milly until each is set free at age 31. |
| 1847 | Watters | Benedict | Gough | Harry | Note $212.00 | Charlotte-25 until free in 1848; Wesley-15, Caroline-6 and Sam-4 slave for life. |
| 1848 | Kenney | John | Bond- Colored | Corbin | One Cent | One Negro child Sarah Jane-8 , Corbin Bond's daughter. |
| 1848 | Johnson | Wm. & Mathew | Johnson | SARAH | Love & affect | Negro Harriet & children: Bill & Mary Jane. |
| 1849 | McGaw | Robert | Martin | Daniel | $250.00 | Negro slave Sidney-14 to serve until age 35. |
| 1850 | Street | William | Street | St Clair | $300.00 | One Negro slave Mahaly Thomas age 30. |

## SLAVE SALES

| Date | Seller First Name | Seller Last Name | Buyer First Name | Buyer Last Name | Price | Transaction |
|------|-------------------|------------------|------------------|-----------------|-------|-------------|
| 1850 | John | Ward | Sam'l | Pyle- Balt Cty | Due $40.00 | One Negro boy Lan. |
| 1851 | Elizabeth H. | Bussey | Elizabeth S. | Bussey | Love & affect | One Negro Ann, age 22. |
| 1851 | Benedict | Hanson | Walter | Harwood | $336.00 | Negro Cassandra-25 & her children: William-7 & John-5. |
| 1852 | Sarah | Amos | Absolom | Galloway | $400.00 | Negro Henetta-25 & her children: Henry-10, Wesley-7, Laura-7mos. |
| 1852 | Henry | Guyton | Thos. | Fortune- Balt.Co | $150.00 | Negro boy Samuel, age 5. |
| 1852 | Robert | Holland | Charles | Christy- Colored | $1.00 | Negro Mary Christy, who cannot be manumitted as she is over 45 years of age. |
| 1852 | Timothy | Keen | Aquila & B.H. | Keen | $400.00 | Services of Chas. Heath until freed in 10 yrs at age 36. |
| 1852 | Robert | Nelson | Harriet | Knolen | $40.50 | One black boy named Merryman. |
| 1853 | John | Murphy | Michael | Christie | $250.00 | Susan Lewis, slave for life. |
| 1853 | Samuel | Sutton | Eliz. & Martha | Howard | $375.00 | Negro Harriet Paca & her Children: James, Fanny, and Sidney. |

## SLAVE SALES

| Date | Seller Last Name | Seller First Name | Buyer Last Name | Buyer First Name | Price | Transaction |
|------|------------------|-------------------|-----------------|------------------|-------|-------------|
| 1853 | McComas | Mary | Bishop- Colored | Rachel | $100.00 | Following slaves: David-13 Joseph-12, Samuel-8, Rachel 6, Thomas-5, Elzabeth-3, Isiah- 7 mos. |
| 1853 | Scott | Otho | Coals | Isaac W. | $400.00 | Negro girls Jane-13 and Mary-10. |
| 1853 | Pitcock | Benjamin | Guy- Colored | Nancy- Bat. Co | $250.00 | Negroes: Cordelia Guy-30 and her child Charles Henry-1. |
| 1854 | Anderson | Benjamin | Henderson | Andrew | $275.00 | Negro Rachel-10 to serve until age 35- any issue to serve until age 35 and thereafter be free. |
| 1854 | Bosley | Joseph | Johnson | Jarrett | $100.00 | One Negro slave Joshua, age 11. |
| 1854 | Bull | Elizabeth | Bay | Daniel | $425.00 | Negro Harriet Green-to be free in 1870- and her children: Sidney-3 and Frances 1. |
| 1854 | Preston | Elizabeth | Hall | Ann | $1.00 | One Negro girl Nancy Hall, age 6. |
| 1855 | Amos | Abraham | Amos | Eliz. & Ann | $2000.00 | One Negro girl. 4 horses, 2 colts, 7 cows, 15 steers, 10 shoats, 1thrashing machine & horse power, all grain on hand & in field, 2 wagons, ox cart & oxen, all farming utensels, household furniture, all personal goods. |

# SLAVE SALES

| Date | Seller Last Name | Seller First Name | Buyer Last Name | Buyer First Name | Price | Transaction |
|---|---|---|---|---|---|---|
| 1855 | Holloway | Charles | Holloway | Hugh | $450.00 | Colored servant Margaret-25 & her child George-5 mos. |
| 1855 | Hall | Louisa | Brook | James | $400.00 | One Negro man Edward-37. |
| 1855 | Brooks | James | Hall | Adaline | $400.00 | One Negro man Edward-37. |
| 1855 | Jones | Stephen | Bishop | Isaac | $200.00 | Negro Rachal, age 40. |
| 1856 | Fulton | Mishal | Osborn | Susan | $1.00 | Negro girl Henny-15- to serve until age 35. |
| 1857 | Galloway | Absolom | Munnikhysen | Dr. Wm. | $500.00 | One Negro boy named Henry. |
| 1857 | Walker | James | Malcalm | James | $300.00 | Negro Horace Wilmore-22 to serve until age 35. |
| 1858 | Bacon | John | McCormick | James | $200.00 | Negro girl Hannah Harkins until 1880 and no longer. |
| 1858 | Baldwin | Jarrett | Maxwell | John Scott | $1800.00 | Foll. Slaves: Susan Johnson-28 & her children :Amanda-12, Harriet-10, Georgeiana-8, Charles-5, Laura, Charles-5 and Laura-3. |
| 1858 | Anderson | John | Nelson | Robert | $175.00 | Services of Negro Rebeccah for 5 yrs and no longer. |

96

## SLAVE SALES

| Date | Seller Last Name | Seller First Name | Buyer Last Name | Buyer First Name | Price | Transaction |
|------|------------------|-------------------|-----------------|------------------|-------|-------------|
| 1859 | Jarrett | Devereaux | Jarrett | Absolom | $274.00 | One Negro Ann Hunter and sundry goods & chattel. |
| 1859 | Nelson | Joshua | Nelson Wife | Margaret | Value rec. | One slave Harriet-15 & Morey-9; All goods, furn. Etc. in house 30 S. Sharp St., Balto. City & lot it stands on. |
| 1860 | Bull | John & Mary | Bull | William E. | $150.00 | Negro Henry Owens-22 until free in 1872. |
| 1860 | Maulsby | Jane | Mausby | Emily | $1.00 | My slave John upon my death. |
| 1861 | Ashton | William | Ashton | Joseph | $313.00 | Negroes: Mary Kell & Basil Kell; 1 carriage, 2 wagons, 3 horses. |
| 1861 | Webster | Joseph | Bateman | Joseph | $375.00 | Negro Jacob Colerian until 1892. |
| 1863 | Street | St. Clair | Baily | Martha Forges | $5.00 | Negroes Caroline and Lily Jones. |
| 1863 | Hanns | Robert | Archer | Stevenson | $200.00 | Negro Dick Bradford for a term of six years. |
| 1863 | Maxwell | John | Maxwell | Edmond | $265.00 | Negro Amanda and her child Henry; Georginia, Harriet, Charles and 2 young children of Negroe Susan. |
| 1863 | Sappington | John | Sappington | Helen | $5.00 | One Negro boy Thomas Scott Durbin- 10, until free in 1881. |

## SLAVE SALES

| Date | Seller Last Name | Seller First Name | Buyer Last Name | Buyer First Name | Price | Transaction |
|------|------------------|-------------------|-----------------|------------------|-------|-------------|
| 1863 | Scott | Martha & Mary | Spencer | Valentine | $5.00 | Pamela Spencer, wife of Valentine, and her children John and Delia. |

# INDEXES

# INDEX – Sellers, Buyers and Manumitters
## * Indicated as Colored or Free Black

-A-

# INDEX – Sellers, Buyers and Manumitters
## * Indicated as Colored or Free Black

# INDEX – Sellers, Buyers and Manumitters
## * Indicated as Colored or Free Black

# INDEX – Sellers, Buyers and Manumitters
## * Indicated as Colored or Free Black

# INDEX – Sellers, Buyers and Manumitters
## * Indicated as Colored or Free Black

# INDEX – Sellers, Buyers and Manumitters
## * Indicated as Colored or Free Black

# INDEX – Sellers, Buyers and Manumitters
## *Indicated as Colored or Free Black*

# INDEX – Sellers, Buyers and Manumitters
## *Indicated as Colored or Free Black*

## INDEX – Sellers, Buyers and Manumitters
### * Indicated as Colored or Free Black

## INDEX – Sellers, Buyers and Manumitters
### * Indicated as Colored or Free Black

## INDEX – Sellers, Buyers and Manumitters
### * Indicated as Colored or Free Black

# INDEX- Slaves with Surnames

# INDEX- Slaves with Surnames

# INDEX- Slaves with Surnames

## INDEX – Slaves Without Surnames

117

## INDEX – Slaves Without Surnames

118

## INDEX – Slaves Without Surnames

# INDEX – Slaves Without Surnames

# INDEX – Slaves Without Surnames

www.ingramcontent.com/pod-product-compliance
Lightning Source LLC
Chambersburg PA
CBHW071805090426
42737CB00012B/1957